CHRISTOPHER POWELL

Discovering
Cottage
Architecture

D0256283

SHIRE PUBLICATIONS LTD

Contents

1. Introduction 3
2. Early cottages, before 1750 7
3. Georgian vernacular, 1750-1815 23
4. Georgian polite, 1750-1815 36
5. Victorian vernacular, 1815-75 46
6. Victorian polite, 1815-75 81
7. Late cottages, 1875-1914 90
8. Rarity recorded 98
Places to visit 101
Further reading 102
Index 103

The cover photograph is by Cadbury Lamb.

British Library Cataloguing in Publication Data
Powell, Christopher
    Discovering cottage architecture.
    1. Cottages – England – History
    I. Title
    782.3'7'0942 NA7562
    ISBN 0-85263-673-3.

728. 370942 POW

Published in 1996 by Shire Publications Ltd, Cromwell House, Church Street, Princes Risborough, Buckinghamshire HP27 9AA, UK.
Copyright © 1984 by Christopher Powell. First published 1984, reprinted 1987, 1991 and 1996. Number 275 in the Discovering series.
ISBN 0 85263 673 3.

Printed in Great Britain by CIT Printing Services, Press Buildings, Merlins Bridge, Haverfordwest, Pembrokeshire SA61 1XF.

1. Introduction

Cottages are one of the most popular of all building types. They need praise less than protection, which comes through understanding. The aim of this book is to help understanding by describing cottage architecture in a social and economic context. The scope is from the oldest survivors to the early twentieth century, in England and Wales. A firm dividing line between cottages and houses is difficult to draw. Cottages are assumed to be small, old and where poor people lived in the country. The upper size limit is taken to be three bedrooms, six main rooms altogether, and a floor area of about 90 square metres (970 square feet). These features give a rough idea, but no single feature is necessary, or sufficient, to make a cottage. The definition is unavoidably loose, recalling Lewis Carroll: 'When *I* use a word it means just what I choose it to mean — neither more nor less.'

The rich variety of cottages is a reason for their powerful appeal. Most looked diverse when new and have grown more so with age. Hands and brains were what once fashioned all cottages, no matter what may have altered them since. It follows that one way in which to approach the variety of cottages is through the people who built and occupied them. Those who decided to build, and their reasons, will explain much. They may have intended to attract the workforce of a farm or mill, adorn an important view, gain income or prestige, or help the poor. The builder, whether the same person or another, may have been a skilled travelling craftsman or a local peasant. Early occupiers ranged from crofters to crossing keepers and from estate foremen to lead miners; all may help to link cottage life and architecture.

A second approach to variety is through the distinction drawn by architectural historians between *vernacular* and *polite* building. Vernacular cottages were commonplace and unpretentious when new. Most were made by non-professional, tradition-bound builders using readily available materials such as rough stone and thatch. Polite cottages were the work of specialist designers aiming at pleasing appearances through widely understood styles. They were open to new ideas and often brought carefully worked materials over long distances. Vernacular cottages probably outnumber polite ones and include many with poorer quality fabrics.

Quality itself is another aspect of cottage variety. Poor quality gave lowest standards of living through smallest floor areas, fewest rooms, lowest headrooms, steepest stairs, smallest windows, scantiest heating and flimsiest construction. Although average quality changed in time and place, there are plenty of

3

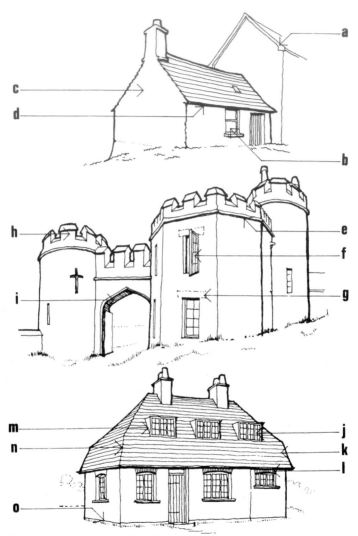

Fig. 1. Vernacular and polite. (Upper) Simple vernacular, Cymmer, Mid Glamorgan. One and a half storey two-room cottage. (Centre) Polite Gothic revival style cottage, Caerhays Castle, Cornwall. (Lower) Polite Edwardian cottage, Uckfield, East Sussex, 1913. Key: a: barge board; b: vertically sliding sash; c: gable; d: eaves; e: string course; f: side-hung casement; g: lintel; h: ornamental parapet; i: Gothic pointed arch; j: dormer; k: mansard roof; l: segmental arch; m: valley; n: hip; o: plinth.

Fig. 2. The limestone belt.

both old high quality cottages and newer poor ones. Steady historical progress should not be assumed.

Regional variety is well known. Clusters of thatched white cob Devon cottages contrast with solitary dark stone Pennine ones. Brightly coloured East Anglian plaster contrasts with Kentish wall tiling and Herefordshire timber. Such differences are rooted in geology, overlain by man's efforts. Weaving, fishing, mining and farming each led to distinctive architecture, enriched by use of local materials. The result was a rough distinction between cottages of the upland north and west and those of the lowland east, midlands and south. Between the two zones runs a great limestone belt from Lincolnshire to Dorset. Regional variety appears to change fastest when travelling across the belt and slowest when parallel to it.

One remaining aspect of variety is the diffusion of novel features and the retreat of obsolescent ones. Many novelties began in the south-east, in towns and in grand architecture. They reached cottages only later and unevenly. Evolutionary change still goes on today, when cottages are adapted to social rise and fall and to changing tastes.

Where a scale is shown in the drawn figures it is in metres; the front door is shown by a broad arrow, and the climb upstairs is

5

shown by a thin arrow.

Many people have helped with this book, some by unlocking for inspection the inner recesses of their homes. Others did much the same in the author's mind. The author expresses thanks to Simon Unwin, and also to Robert Bennett, S. M. Cole, H. F. A. Engleheart, David Grech, Valerie Green, Peter Hunt, G. Kelsey, Jeremy Lowe, I. McGraghan, R. Paterson, Tony Platt, John Powell, Lance Smith, Philip Twentyman, D. E. Wilkins and H. Winney. He is also grateful to the National Museum of Wales (Welsh Folk Museum) for permission to use the Rhostryfan cottage illustration (plate 15); to Ironbridge Gorge Museum Trust for material about Shelton tollhouse and Little Dawley squatter cottage; to Torfaen Museum Trust for material about Pontymoile lock cottage; and to the authors of works listed under Further Reading.

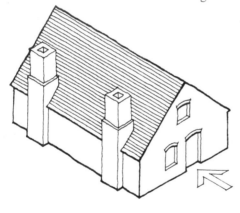

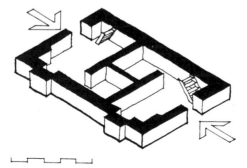

Fig. 3. Barn adapted into two cottages, Llanvetherine, Gwent. Each cottage has four rooms (inner ones without direct lighting).

2. Early cottages, before 1750

Cottagers: who and where

Many cottages seen today were regarded in the past as no less than grand houses. All the oldest surviving examples began life as the homes of people of means. For this reason they need to be distinguished from true cottages which were built originally for humble people. In this chapter, formerly grand houses will be considered in outline before moving to the earliest true cottages.

The population needing a place to live was small by modern standards. In the middle of the sixteenth century there were only about three and a quarter million people in England and Wales. Gradual growth took the total to about six million by the middle of the eighteenth century, of whom half or more were labouring poor. Building activity needed to add to the national housing stock was moderate. Some building took place because a slow and halting increase in national wealth improved housing quality. Sometimes building activity quickened with a growth of trade or succession of good harvests, and at other times activity was only sluggish. Another cause of house building was the occasional movement of people from one place to another, but probably the biggest stimulus was the frequent replacement of flimsy huts 'such as a man may build within three or four hours'. These cabins lasted no more than a human generation or two before they needed rebuilding. Permanence in housing, taken for granted today, was long confined to the homes of the well off. The geographical distribution of population and houses was scattered, with no large towns except London, and most people in the more fertile country of the south, east and midlands. These regions supported many agricultural labourers as well as the prosperous woollen villages. Elsewhere, in the north and far west, the population was thin, standards of living were generally lower, and cottages fewer and mainly poor.

Early occupiers of formerly grand houses, now regarded as cottages, were separated from true cottagers by their wealth and status, which were above the poor and below the gentry. Most were small landowners and farmers or yeomen, with some smaller tradesmen and merchants. Most avoided privation, but seldom had surplus with which to indulge in great display about their homes. True cottagers lived precariously by labouring for others, mostly on farms, or by scraping their living from smallholdings or commons. In Stuart times and earlier many of their class lived with their employers rather than in separate households. Communal living slowly declined and, as the number of poor increased, a growing proportion lived in cottages. By the eighteenth century landless labourers were a large part of the population. Their standards of living were not

7

far above subsistence and most homes were bare and comfortless. Those with animals might live near or even with them — a valuable source of warmth in winter. At worst, when crops or work failed, and among large families, cottagers faced poverty. In good times, when there were few dependants, enough work and a strong supporting community, there could be an appearance of ease.

Formerly grand house form

The following short outline of formerly grand houses is limited by their marginal status as cottages. Deeper study of them properly belongs in the field of vernacular architecture. The starting point in looking at house types is the medieval open hall (*hall house*). This large room open to the apex of the roof was the centre of life for an entire household, from lord to servants. Typically it was high enough for the same roof to extend over some flanking two-storey accommodation at both ends of the hall. Most halls were entered from a passage which ran across the building between two opposing external doors. Originally, a central hearth heated the hall and blackened it with smoke, but more controlled fires came later, first with smoke hood and then fireplace and chimney. At one end of the hall, on the far side of the passage, were the service rooms of buttery and pantry and at the other end were the solar and private rooms. These rooms were usually small in early hall houses and larger in later ones. Over a long life, halls slowly moved down the social scale before they finally fell obsolete from the middle of the sixteenth century. In heyday and decline they were an architectural expression of a social and economic order. The expression varied, with some halls quite small and rudely built and others large and made of massive timbers. Among the finest examples are *Wealden houses*, named after the locality near which most are found. They have generous timber frames and overhanging first-floor walls which flank the flush walls of the hall itself, giving a distinctive wide recessed front.

In decline many hall houses sooner or later became suitable candidates for conversion. Halls were often divided by the insertion of a first floor, partitions and extra windows. A once proud Wealden house could be divided into three cottages, one in the former service rooms, another in the private rooms and a third in the hall. Piecemeal alterations so transformed some houses that their original identity was lost, sometimes to the surprise of modern researchers.

New house types did not develop in a clear succession of different forms, each replacing the one before. Instead, many changes were confused and erratic. From the early sixteenth century, houses of two full storeys throughout, or at least one

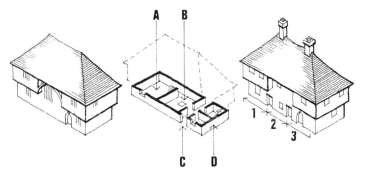

Fig. 4. Wealden hall house. (Left) As built. (Centre) Plan. A: private room. B: hall. C: cross passage. D: service rooms. (Right) As converted into three cottages.

storey and an attic, began to appear in the south-east. Elsewhere, older forms, more closely related to open halls, continued to be built. When the two-storey houses eventually spread beyond the south-east, later in the sixteenth century, most were smaller than the pioneers. House sizes and types increased during the seventeenth century, as did the number which have survived to the present day.

A readily identified house type is the *longhouse*. It has no standard form, but a key feature was that it was occupied by both people and animals. Longhouses were divided into two by a through passage, reached by doorways in both long sides, in a way similar to hall houses. On one side of the passage was the living space and on the other side the byre. The living space might be of one or two storeys, or one and a half storeys, that is having an attic over the ground floor. Typical ground-floor living space was a heated main room, nearest to the passage, and an inner room opening off the main room, furthest from the byre. In some earlier longhouses the living space and byre were only flimsily divided, but many later examples were divided by a chimney backing on to the through passage. For drainage purposes the living-space floor generally was higher than that in the byre.

Longhouses were an ancient upland house type, where hill farmers needed to shelter cattle. Some of the oldest survivors are in Hereford and Worcester, and others were built in Devon, many in the century after about 1550. As they fell from favour in the south west they began to be built in the far north, often in larger sizes. A Scottish border variant of the combined human and animal shelter was the defensive bastle house, in which

9

living space was built over, instead of alongside, the byre. Later alterations to longhouses have made their interpretation problematical. They could easily be converted into semi-detached pairs of cottages by blocking a doorway in the passage partition and adding a fireplace in the former byre. Some longhouses (and others) instead were converted into farm buildings, perhaps later to be rehabilitated back into cottages.

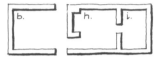 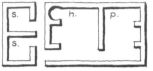

Fig. 5. Plans. (Left) Longhouse. (Right) Through-passage house. b: byre. h: hall. i: inner room. s: service room. p: parlour.

Another form of house divided by a passage is common in many regions. The *through-passage type* had on the ground floor a main room which may still be called a hall or, later, a hall-kitchen. It was divided by a passage from the service rooms, rather than the byre, as in longhouses. At the far end of the main room, tucked away furthest from the entrance, was the parlour. As communal living went out of fashion the main room lost importance to the parlour, which gave greater privacy. Through-passage houses fell from favour in the south-east at almost the same time as halls. In many other places through-passage houses went on being built until well into the seventeenth century and after. Of the many variants which appeared, some had chimneys which backed on to the passage and others, particularly larger and lowland houses, had chimneys placed away from the passage. In the south-west some chimneys projected boldly from the front walls, where they served as status symbols. Most through-passage houses which eventually declined to become regarded as cottages probably were subdivided. Like many older houses of all kinds, some were extended by raising the walls and roof. Where cramped attics were lifted to full storey height, a horizontal joint or change of wall material often remains as evidence.

Through-passage houses were followed by what are called *undivided houses*, which lacked a passage. Again, they were entered at about the mid-point of the long wall, but in this case the door gave access to a lobby. In front of the door was a flank wall of the chimney, on one side was the main room door and on the other side was the parlour door. Inside the main room were further doors to the smaller service rooms beyond. Other versions of the undivided house had no separate lobby, but instead were entered directly into one of the rooms. Undivided house plans arose as a result of a growing distinction between the farmer's family and his labourers. The old through passage had lessened the inconvenience to the farmer that arose from the use of the house by labourers as a work centre. Now the passage became less useful because more labourers lived and worked away from the farmer's household. These changes occurred first in the south-east, where the undivided house came earliest. It spread during the seventeenth century but remained most common in the lowlands. With greater numbers came various adaptations and fluidity in the uses and names of the different rooms. The type may often be recognised by looking at the front elevation, where the door is seen to be aligned closely with a chimney above it.

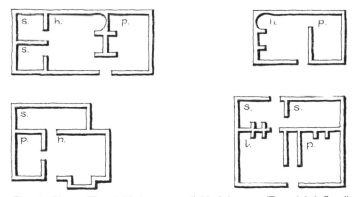

Fig. 6. Plans. (Top left) Larger undivided house. (Top right) Small undivided house. (Lower left) House with outshut. (Lower right) Double pile house. s: service room. h. hall or main room. p. parlour. l: living room.

Later houses had kitchens, dairies, more upstairs rooms and bigger living spaces, often arranged in complex T- and L-shaped plans. Rear extensions, or outshuts, which reached part way or entirely across the widths of houses were provided initially or added later. Some of these quite imposing houses were eventually split into groups of cottages. Undivided houses with outshuts were only a short step from the ultimate development, in which living spaces were displayed at the front and kitchen and other working service rooms were banished to the back. These double-pile houses were two main rooms wide and deep and had formal symmetrical fronts. Most were too large to be regarded today as cottages, and probably not many were subdivided.

True cottage form

Early cottages originally built for labourers and those with little land are far more scarce than formerly grand houses of similar date. Very few surviving true cottages were built before the middle of the seventeenth century and most are in the lowlands. The great majority which once existed has been lost because flimsy construction decayed long ago. The remains of slight cottages of sticks and mud, which were rebuilt frequently on the same sites, have been found by archaeological excavation. These crude shelters are likely to have been put up throughout the sixteenth century and after. Some appeared on roadsides and common land, where they had doubtful right to be. Many must have disappeared equally quickly through the effects of storm or, if the encroachment was resented, man. On the other hand, some survived long enough to gain a foothold, be improved with more durable materials and last to the present.

The poorest of the squatters' cottages were little more than overnight shelters or like the charcoal burners' huts of recent times. Others were low, one-room windowless dwellings, from which smoke from a central hearth escaped through the doorway. As Celia Fiennes wrote in 1698, many were but 'sad little hutts' and furnishings were sparse. They might only amount to some makeshift scraps of wooden furniture, a water jar and some straw bedding or a flock mattress. Cottagers spent much of their time in the open air, where they could cook and eat as well as work. Services as understood today were unknown and water was fetched from a well or stream, perhaps at some distance, and wastes of all kinds were scattered around the cottage. Where there was a garden it was a utilitarian source of food rather than decorative pleasure. Plants which did not help to fill stomachs had little place in lives near the level of subsistence. Some plain words of 1682, quoted by Iorwerth Peate, describe a view which seems not to have been unusual: 'a Dunghill modell'd into the shape of a cottage, whose outward surface . . . appear'd not unlike a great blot of Cow-turd . . .'

Not all cottages, now lost, can have been as dismal as this. Higher standards could be reached, particularly where family earnings from farming were augmented by cottage industry. This prospered in the earlier eighteenth century and included chair turning, knitting, lacemaking, nailmaking, spinning and weaving. Families who did such work might afford better cottages with two or more rooms and several storeys. Access to attic space over all or part of the ground floor could be by a ladder stair. Although steep to climb, it took up less space and was more easily made than orthodox stairs. The old central hearth, which blackened the interior (and inhabitants), was replaced first by a hood and later by a fireplace and chimney, following the same sequence as that in wealthy homes. As Boswell remarked, 'The philosophers, when they placed happiness in a cottage, supposed cleanliness and no smoke.' Another sign of rising standards was that sticks and mud began to give way to more lasting materials.

The small minority of early true cottages which survive must be among the best of the original stock. Their forms are variations upon a simple theme, although original fabric may not be easy to distinguish from later alterations. Siting appears more or less arbitrary to the modern eye, with cottages facing on to, away from or siding roads. Neither was there much evident concern with sunlight or direction of prevailing winds. Plans may be rectangular or square, and most headrooms are low. Internal dimensions are seldom more than about 6.5 metres (20 feet) or less than about 3 metres (9 feet), with most examples not near either extreme. The resulting floor areas are small but compare well with modern caravans. There may be one storey, one and a half, two, or even two storeys plus attic for some better quality examples. Original windows are likely to be few and small, and those on upper floors often are in a gable or dormer or at eaves level. In many cases the ground floor is or was once partitioned into two main rooms. Outshuts are common, either as part of the original building or as an early addition. The position of the fireplace and chimney varies, in some cases being in an external wall, probably a gable if the cottage is of stone. In other cases it may be in a party wall, backing on to the fireplace of an adjacent cottage. Some rooms were unheated and the sole fireplace, where cooking took place over a wood fire, is a generous width, like the flue above it. Many original chimneys have been replaced because of decay. Today once common ladder stairs are all but extinct and most original surviving stairs probably are spiral or half-turn types. Many were positioned next to the chimney, although the more grand stair turret projecting from an outside wall is not unknown.

There are no easy or infallible distinctions between true cottages and formerly grand houses, although several pointers exist. Original buildings must not be confused with later alterations and reused components. The first pointer is that true cottages are always small, but many formerly grand houses are relatively big and have many rooms. The headroom in true cottages is likely to be low but may not be so in formerly grand houses. Another pointer is decorative carving in stone and timber, particularly on roof members, windows, fireplace lintels and floor beams. The presence of more than the simplest carving is a sign that the building was once seen as better than a cottage. True cottagers seldom had enough means for more than a bare minimum, in building as in much else. For this reason the more ornate, durable and substantial the building, the more likely it is to be a formerly grand house.

Building fabric

Timber frames were the widely favoured early method of building. Cruck timbers were a form of ancient and noble origins, which filtered down to the level of humble buildings by the end of the sixteenth century. *Cruck construction* consists of pairs of large inclined timbers which rise to meet at an apex. The timbers may be curved, straight or elbowed at eaves level. They are joined by a horizontal tie beam or collar, to make an A frame. The space between two pairs of crucks is called a bay, across which horizontal purlin beams span to support the roof. One bay, which might measure about 4 by 4 metres (12 by 12 feet), was enough for a cottage, but bigger houses needed more bays. Where possible, crucks were of stout oak, but many cottagers had to make do with less. As suitable oak became scarce, so ways of using smaller timbers were found. One way was to build up each cruck blade out of several pieces which were jointed and pegged together. Another was for crucks to rise from bases set up off the ground in masonry walls, rather than from ground level, thereby saving timber and lessening decay due to damp. Crucks survive in a thin scattering outside eastern areas, although many are altered or concealed by later work. Groups of them may be seen around Weobley (Hereford and Worcester); Ashleworth and Dymock (Gloucestershire) and Harwell (Oxfordshire).

Crucks are not the most common form of timber framing. Much more usual are frames which are discontinuous at eaves level, that is, with separate wall and roof members. The weight

Fig. 7. Timber frames. (Left) Cruck, Weobley (Hereford and Worcester), early sixteenth century or before. Some original secondary vertical and horizontal members have been removed. (Right) Box frame, Eardisland (Hereford and Worcester).

of the roofs of some buildings of this type is taken to the ground through transverse frames spaced at intervals along the length of the building. This form is known as *post and truss construction,* of which the resulting bays show some structural likeness to cruck building. The alternative to post and truss was *box frame construction,* in which roof loads were carried on framed side walls, without the appearance of bays. The term 'box frame' is also applied loosely to any timber-framed building not having crucks.

Fig. 8. Timber frame types. (Left upper) Small framing. (Left centre) Large framing with braces. (Left lower) Close studding. (Right) Large framing, with brick ground floor facing, Penshurst (Kent).

There are three kinds of box frame walling, one of which is *large framing,* built commonly from the middle of the fifteenth century. It has square or near-square storey-height panels within which may be diagonal braces or decorative timbers. *Close studding* differs from this in having closely spaced storey-height vertical members. It was the most esteemed and extravagant pattern of walling and is most often found in the south and east. The poorer relation of close studding, most often found in timber-framed cottages and in the midlands and west, is *small framing.* In this there are two panels for each storey height and in some superior cases bold repetitive decoration of star, herringbone or other pattern. Small framing became common in the fifteenth century and, like other box framing, continued to be built until the end of the seventeenth century. As a rule, the more massive and closely spaced the timbers, the more grand was the original building. Some wall frames have upper floor walls which are jettied, that is they overhang the face of the wall

15

below. This feature, which gives structural advantages, makes good use of tight sites and protects walls from rain, was more common on grand and urban buildings than true cottages. Wall frames commonly rest on low stone or brick walls (or plinths) which help to keep the lowest horizontal timbers (or cills) dry and hence less subject to decay. Frame members usually were made of freshly felled oak, which is easier to work than seasoned material, which becomes very hard. The carpenter assembled the frame on the site after he had first fashioned the members in his yard. This form of prefabrication was helped by incised identity numbers, sometimes still visible, on the joints. Many timbers warped and twisted as they dried out, making buildings lean and sag in unexpected but not necessarily harmful ways.

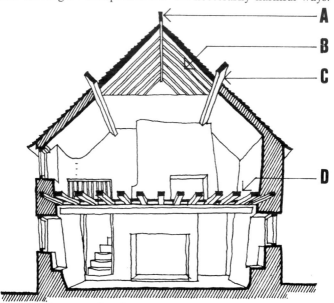

Fig. 9. Roof construction. Section through stone cottage, sixteenth or seventeenth century, Ampney St Peter (Gloucestershire). A: ridge. B: rafters. C: purlin beam. D: floor joists. Original eaves were lower and roof pitch steeper.

Many original roof structures have been lost for, like chimneys, they are vulnerable to decay. Surviving major roof structures in formerly grand houses show great variety and ingenuity in the use of crown post, king post and other types. The best examples are one of the great glories of the architecture of the period. In true cottages the roof structures are far more simple since spans and opportunities for display were small. At most, structures consist of the following rough-hewn timber parts: rafters, or members inclined from eaves up to ridge; a truss, or triangulated members made of two stout rafters linked in the shape of an A by a horizontal tie or collar, to prevent spreading; and purlins, or beams between gable walls, supporting the rafters near their mid-point. The simplest roof structures have only rafters (possibly with collars), but better building practice and larger spans employ purlins to support the rafters. More advanced structures also have a truss, or principal rafter assembly, to support the purlins. Typical later roof structures, like later wall frames, used smaller timbers, apparently because of scarcity. Shipbuilding and ironmaking competed with building for remaining supplies and cottage builders had to make do as best they could. Old timbers from demolished buildings were reused and may be identified by redundant joint slots and peg holes, which appear in random positions. Despite a common belief, timbers appear seldom, if ever, to have been taken from old ships. By the eighteenth century timber members were straight, slender and widely spaced in minor buildings and abandoned for walls of major ones. Carpenters had been forced to work nearer to the limit of strength of the material and to forsake the earlier attractive but wasteful oversizing. Mean timbers were also used in earlier times, but most have been lost by decay, giving a false impression today that the oldest work was rarely mean.

The panels within timber frames commonly were filled with *wattle and daub*. This consists of light timber verticals let at intervals into holes in horizontal frame members, woven with wattles and daubed with a mix of clay, dung and chopped straw, or similar. Lifespan and draughtproofing of panels were improved by coats of limewash or plaster either on the daub alone or also over the frame. The 'magpie' appearance of black-painted timber contrasted with white infill seems to date only from the nineteenth century, before which most timber was left in its attractive natural state. Sometimes brick was used instead of wattle and daub, either initially or as a replacement. *Brick nogging*, as it is known, was arranged in casual random patterns or decorative herringbone arrangements. Another method of enclosing timber frames was to spread lime plaster over wooden laths fixed to the outside of the frame. On some later higher quality work, mainly in the east, the plaster surface was moulded in decorative patterns and images, in a practice known as *pargeting*. A far cruder method, of which a few Lincolnshire examples survive, was to build large wall panels of mud stiffened by encased wooden staves.

Fig. 10. *Plastered timber frame. Four-room south Suffolk cottage with lean-to addition.*

Mud and stave building may be said to be a form midway between timber framing and mass unbaked earth. The plainest unbaked earth construction was turf, a now vanished material. A more advanced form is *cob,* which is one of the names given to walls of mixed clay, straw, chalk and small stones, used in varying proportions. Cob walls were built up out of a series of rough horizontal courses, or lifts, each about 600 millimetres (2 feet) high. Except when in decay, these courses are hidden by protective layers of plaster or whitewash, which, with stone or brick plinths, are needed to prevent damage by moisture. Wall thicknesses range from a little less than 600 millimetres (2 feet) to 1.2 metres (4 feet) or more. The plastic nature of cob produced rounded rather than sharp corners, quite small and few openings and wavy rather than perfectly plane wall faces. Many existing cob buildings were put up in the eighteenth century, although some are older. Once cob was widespread and today it is still widely scattered, with concentrations in Devon and parts of adjoining counties. Around Haddenham (Buckinghamshire) is a local variant known as *wichert.*

Stone was regarded as superior to cob, and it did not come within the limited grasp of cottagers much before the middle of the seventeenth century. Even then it did so only in prosperous areas which had suitable stone, pre-eminently the Cotswolds. Generally it was impracticable to carry stone very far for cottage building and so, once surface supplies were used up, small quarries were opened. Gradually, masons were forced to use more stones which were either hard to cut or difficult to bond together or presented other practical problems. They included

18

hard sandstones, flint and chalk block, or clunch. Different colours, textures, sizes and manners of jointing and laying are an endless source of visual interest and variety. Masonry was a more skilled job than cob building, which could be carried out by the intending occupiers. The simplest stone walls were made of rubble of random size and shape, usually with the largest stones near the foot. Cornerstones (or quoins) needed to be large and suitably shaped for stability. The strength of a wall depended largely on the bonding agent, which could be mud, clay mortar or, in later and superior work, lime mortar. Where possible, random rubble was rejected in favour of coursed rubble laid in ordered courses with continuous horizontal joints. Typical wall thicknesses are about 450 millimetres (18 inches) to 600 millimetres (2 feet), with later higher quality work in easily cut stone likely to be thinner than earlier poor work in hard stone. Accurately cut and jointed stone (or ashlar), found in superior buildings, was little used in cottages because it was too costly. At most, there might be simple carved chamfers around window and door openings. Even in favoured limestone regions like the Cotswolds, timber lintels might be used as a cheaper alternative to stone.

Fig. 11. Stone bonding. (Left) Random rubble. (Centre) Coursed rubble with ashlar quoins. (Right) Chequered stone and flint.

Brick was also regarded as a high quality material and it did not filter down to the cottage level until about half a century after stone. It began to appear in lowland stone-free areas from about the late seventeenth century. Before then it was limited to minor special uses like plinths, quoins, timber-frame infill, fireplaces and chimneys, in which heat resistance and ease of laying were important. Early bricks varied widely in size, shape and colour, even within the same batch. This was because they were hand-made and often fired in improvised clamps on the building site, where the clay was dug, rather than in permanent kilns. Some bricks were fired hard and dark, while others were underfired, making them soft and attractively warm and mellow in colour. Uneven bricks gave uneven joints, which heightened

19

the heavily textured, random appearance of finished walls. Yet, where needed, accuracy was possible as, for example, in complicated patterns of bonding on gables in·eastern counties, known as *tumbling-in*. This is bricklaying on the vulnerable upper surface of gable walls, at right angles to the roof pitch, rather than horizontally, to improve durability at a weak point.

Fig. 12. Brick tumbling-in on gable. Holmpton (Humberside).

To place different wall materials into neat categories is to ignore improvisations and apparent oddities in cottage building. Many single cottages when new had a mixture of materials, which was added to in later alterations. For instance, front and back walls could be timber-framed, infilled in several ways and partly plastered over, while gable walls could be flint, perhaps mixed with brick. The more complicated the history is, the greater the range of materials: timber jetties concealed by later brick cladding; ancient crucks partly removed and replaced by stone; and chimneys patched, heightened and renewed several times. The society which gave rise to early cottages was both poorer and less tidy-minded than today's. Materials were used as they came to hand, and few things so lacked value as not to be worth reusing.

Replacement and renewal were the rule rather than the exception for roof finishes. *Thatch* once dominated, but where it survives now it is not original, for even the best is not expected to outlive a human lifespan by much. The most common materials were reeds, straw and heather, all of which were light in weight and could be conveniently formed into the intricate shapes of roof valleys, hips and gables. Various other roof finishes were used on higher quality work and some must have begun to appear on cottages later in the period. There were various sorts of *stone slates* including the widely admired Cotswold limestone. This was laid in graduated courses, smallest at the ridge and largest at the eaves, on steep roof pitches of fifty degrees or more. Where less workable sandstones were found, more massive flags were laid at pitches of about thirty degrees. Flags were less easily cut than limestone, so roof shapes were kept to simple planes, without difficult hip and valley junctions. Roofing stone was kept in place by oak pegs or occasionally by small animal bones.

Other alternatives to thatch were *shingles* and, far more widespread, the two types of clay tiles. *Plain tiles* came first, with a history parallel to the bricks which were made alongside them. Being lighter, tiles could be carried over greater distances than bricks, making them probably one of the first important finished products in cottages to be traded widely. Plain tiles measuring about 250 by 150 millimetres (10 by 6 inches) were pegged in place in overlapping courses. Like limestone, they suited steep rather than shallow roof pitches and could be fitted to intricate hips and valleys. *Pantiles* are larger and lighter than plain tiles and may be laid on lower pitched roofs, although hip and valley junctions present difficulties. The first pantiles were imported from the Low Countries in the late seventeenth century and British-produced ones followed early in the next century.

The ground floors of most true cottages were earth, often mixed with a bonding agent such as bullocks' blood, lime or clay. Bricks and stone flags are likely to have appeared in only a few superior cottages. Early first floors were of large-section timber joists, with parallel boards filling the narrow spaces between. Later examples were more like current practice, with smaller joists, and boards which spanned in the opposite direction. Joists were gradually changed from square or near-square laid face down, to rectangular and laid on edge. Typical floorboard widths narrowed over the period and elm and fir increasingly were substituted for oak. In the east midlands some first floors were made of plaster, about 50 millimetres (2 inches) thick, spanning between timbers. Generally, ceilings were not originally provided, and this made upper rooms cold in winter, although some

Fig. 13. Roof finishes. (Left) Stone slates laid in graduated courses. (Centre) Plain clay tiles. (Right) Clay pantiles.

warmth would have passed up between the boards from the rooms below.

The construction of some partitions was like that of external walls, especially where roof or floor loadings were carried on them. Many non-structural partitions were mere short-lived screens, but some were closely spaced timber verticals grooved to receive vertical boards, the whole being fixed to horizontals at head and foot. Many later partitions were more slender than early ones and less likely to be made of oak. Windows and doors are prone to early replacement, so originals are often missing. Early windows had fabric instead of costly glass and were not made to open. From the early eighteenth century glass began to reach the better cottages, and opening lights began to appear. Use was made of metals, timber-frame side-hung casements and timber horizontal (Yorkshire) sliders. Shutters were common, and doors were battened, or built up from vertical boards, rather than panelled.

3. Georgian vernacular, 1750-1815

Cottage needs and provision

Rural life began to change more rapidly after the mid eighteenth century. The population of around six million in 1750 grew to nine million by 1800, four fifths of whom lived in the country. The proportion of working people who were in agriculture fell, although as yet this reflected growth outside agriculture rather than decline within it. The tranquil England of Parson Woodforde went on its unquestioning way, in a changing world.

Agricultural enclosures were one of the most visible changes. The open field system of small unfenced strips of land scattered over the parish was being transformed by Parliamentary Enclosure Acts, which reached a peak between 1800 and 1815. Where the transformation was greatest, in Northamptonshire and its surroundings, a new planned landscape of rectangular fields, hedges and copses emerged, to the benefit of larger farmers. Many unfortunate and inefficient smallholders faced hardship through loss of commons and an inability to afford fencing, but the gains in crop yield enabled a growing population to eat. Rising food prices encouraged cultivation of ever more marginal uplands and wastes while on fertile lowlands landowners improved their estates. Followers of men like 'Turnip' Townshend tried new farming methods and others founded new mills, mines and workshops in open countryside.

Amid the change, old motives for cottage building remained and were augmented. There was a need for new cottages to replace decay and populate reclaimed wasteland. Faster population growth brought a new urgency to housing need, met partly by altering old outbuildings and barns. Old village farmhouses were subdivided into cottages when their owners left them for new outlying farmsteads among the enclosed fields. New motives for cottage building were the welfare of occupiers and the display and prestige to be had from cottage aesthetics. In the half century after 1750 income per head nearly doubled, making possible a view beyond mere survival and creating some opportunities for better housing. Since few cottagers themselves received a proportionate share of growing wealth, it usually fell to others to initiate building.

A few people who decided to build were freeholders who built for themselves and some were squatters on wastelands which survived enclosure. Others built as investment, selling outright or letting to tenants, and others again were employers who built to rent to their workforces. Despite the myth of 'the good old days', most cottage occupiers still lived precarious lives. Although standards of living had improved in the earlier

23

eighteenth century, deterioration set in after the 1760s and worsened after 1790 with bad harvests and rising wartime prices. The population pressed ever more relentlessly against the means of subsistence and the stock of cottages. Probably the majority of cottagers were farm labourers, the most comfortable of whom had a garden or the use of common land. A minority were skilled artisans and craftsmen such as wheelwrights and blacksmiths or were employed in mineral workings, textile and other outwork which had so far resisted transfer to factories. The head of household might spend part of a season in the fields and part in a brickyard or quarry while his wife was at home plaiting, spinning or weaving and the children scared birds or picked stones in the fields.

Conditions in the south seem to have been best; in the west they probably deteriorated, while in the north they probably improved from the lowest level. General building standards seem likely to have become slightly better. Improvement was not found everywhere, or in all respects, but permanent materials probably were more usual in cottages in 1815 than in 1750. Within regions, housing conditions in adjacent parishes could differ widely. Repairs depended on the landlord, except in the case of a minority of cottage owner-occupiers. Some parishes were owned by one landlord, so his attitude and wealth could decide the fate of a whole village. He might embark upon rebuilding and improvement or, equally, he might (until 1865) evict and demolish, to lessen his liability for poor rates. Hapless cottagers could be forced from their 'close' parish to crowd into the nearest 'open' one. In 'open' parishes land ownership was fragmented and cottages might be rented there; otherwise there was the common or the town. 'Close' parishes were where cottage design for large landowners was likely to be carried out by specialists. Most of the resulting architecture was polite, while many 'open' parishes were vernacular strongholds.

Form and fabric

Cottage building methods and local character were probably at their most varied in the early nineteenth century. Newer durable materials were added to the range of temporary ones, as yet without displacing them. Brick made more progress than other materials, despite a brick tax from 1784. In this it was helped by better road and water transport for finished goods and coal for firing them. Particular plan types showed few signs of becoming universal, although more small groups and rows of similar cottages began to appear. These beginnings of repetition reflected the growing size of business workforces and settlements. Cottages continued to be built with one, one and a half, two and more storeys, and some had one room on each floor and

Fig. 14. Regional map.

others had two, or sometimes more. Many four-room cottages had wide frontages rather than narrow, with rooms side by side and the entrance in a long side. Narrow frontage plans with rooms one behind the other and the entrance in a short side seem likely to have been most used in repetitive cottages built in short rows. The best cottages had improvements such as internal plastering, ceilings, stone or brick floors and bigger windows, more of which were made to open, often as timber side-hung casements. Superior vertically sliding sashes were confined to the very best work, as were panelled doors. Glass became more

25

common although much was inferior crown glass with 'bull's eye' optical imperfections.

Further description of cottage fabric follows on a regional basis, to outline the richness of local vernacular. There is neither enough space nor sufficient detailed fieldwork to attempt a comprehensive view of architectural character. Many minor features, as well as some points of comparison between regions, must here pass unnoted.

South-east England

Cottage quality in this region, and particularly in Kent, was at its best. The range of wall and roof materials was almost unrivalled and the development of details like chimneys and porches was well advanced, and their upkeep remains good today. Former poorly built 'tottering hovels' have now gone, leaving many cottages which show a sense of well-being which comes from warm brick and tile colours, smart paintwork and well stocked gardens. Mellow orange and red bricks appear widely and may be seen at their best in quiet chequer and diaper wall patterns. Red stretcher bricks (long face visible) were used alternately with blue or grey header bricks (short face visible). Joints became thinner and less uneven than hitherto and brick bonding less random and more ordered.

The imposition of the brick tax encouraged some substitute materials such as sawn imported softwood wall framing used in slender uprights 450 millimetres (18 inches) apart. Commonly this was clad with warm-coloured plain rectangular tiles which give a rich wall texture like that of a plain tiled roof. Mathematical or brick tiles, shaped to look almost indistinguishable from bricks when fixed in place, also might be used, for example in the vicinity of Lewes (East Sussex). Another wall cladding was horizontal timber weatherboarding, at first natural elm, but later more regularly shaped painted pine. Assorted yellow, brown and grey sandstones were used where they could be found, sometimes with a practice unusual outside the region, known as galleting. This is the insertion of small pieces of stone into freshly laid mortar joints, supposedly to strengthen the joints and add visual interest. A poorer material which survives more commonly from the later eighteenth century is flint. This material was laborious to use and, being prone to structural instability, was commonly reinforced with brick at quoins and in alternating horizontal lacing courses. Similar brick lacing courses were used where other stone was of poor quality. The wide range of regional walling materials and their different practical qualities often led them to be mixed in single buildings. Many cottages have a characteristic 'waist band', with lower walls of one material, often brick, and upper walls of another, say tile hanging.

Many roofs are covered with plain tiles matching those on the walls, but weathered a darker colour. Thatch survives well over the region, being helped by a dry climate and the favourable attitude of many modern owners towards preservation of architectural character. Many roofs are hipped and some are swept down boldly in a catslide to low eaves at the side or rear. Others have quite different thick heavy Horsham stone slates on simple low roof pitches.

An idea of accommodation standards in about 1780 comes from a row recorded in East Malling (Kent) by Mercer. They were built of timber weatherboarding on a light timber frame. Each cottage had a heated front room about 5.0 by 3.3 metres (16 feet by 10 feet 6 inches), reached directly from the front door. A smaller back room opened off the main room and contained the stairs, which gave access to one large and one small bedroom on the first floor.

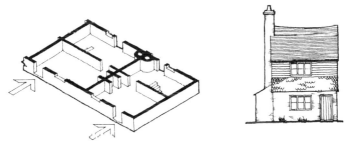

Fig. 15. (Left) Ground-floor plan of two of row of four-room cottages, about 1780, East Malling (Kent). (After E. Mercer.) (Right). Brick and tilehanging near Chiddingstone (Kent).

East Anglia

Builders in this agriculturally rich region worked in the largest area in Britain without good building stone. Slight timber framing was the main alternative, but rather than hanging tiles for cladding they preferred external plaster finished with light colourwash. The appearance of cottages in the flat open landscape is bold and bright, rather as it is south of the Thames. This is in contrast to upland northern and western appearances, where strong landscape encouraged quiet cottages subservient to their surroundings.

A material found in a large inland zone from the late eighteenth century is clay lump. It consists of unfired chalky and sandy mixes cast in blocks about twice the size of bricks. It is

27

vulnerable to damp and must be protected by plaster rendering or brick facing, which generally conceals the material completely except when in decay. Much clay lump is found where poor materials linger longest, in minor outbuildings. The same applies to weatherboarding on light timber framing, often preserved with pitch or tar instead of paint.

The obvious permanent substitute for stone was brick, with pale yellows in the west, mellow reds in the south and more strident colours in the north. The search for other walling materials, often mixed with brick to give stability, led to the use of flint, notably at Brandon (Suffolk), pebbles along the coast and clunch in the north.

The thatching tradition is the strongest and most ornate in Britain, with confident sweeping contours, pointed gables and decorated ridge patterns. Where thatch is absent tiles are used, plain in the south and pantiles further north. Typical roofs have low eaves and attic bedrooms lit by small wedge-shaped dormer windows with roof pitches similar to the main roof, but less steep. Where there are no dormers there may be pairs of small gable wall windows, perhaps flanking a characteristic tapering brick chimney. Continental influence is seen in occasional mansard roofs, in which each roof face has two slopes, the lower one steeper than the upper. Mansards, which give good interior headrooms, began to reach cottages in the later eighteenth century.

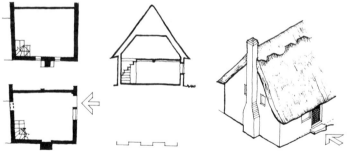

Fig. 16. Timber frame and plaster. Two-room thatched cottage near Stoke-by-Nayland (Suffolk).

Large East Anglian farms with concentrated workforces seem to have led to provision of rows of cottages. Where land holdings were smaller, for example in the poorer fens, many cottages were single or in pairs, as suited a more scattered population. In the early nineteenth century the difference between the best and worst new cottages probably was as marked in this region as anywhere. A near minimal one-up-and-one-down fen cottage of

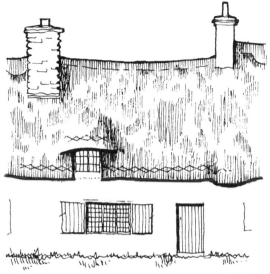

Fig. 17. Limestone rubble and thatch, Great Milton (Oxfordshire).

timber and plaster might cost £30 to build. At the same time a more permanent, but not luxurious, Norfolk flint and pantile cottage with living room, two bedrooms (one unlit) and a lean-to store might cost £65, and about £2 a year to rent, out of an agricultural wage of perhaps £20 a year.

Central England

The long-established Cotswold stone tradition of the centre of the region is flanked by two zones of more mixed materials and practices. Cotswold visual unity, linking walls and roofs, cottages and great houses, villages and landscapes, stems from the local limestone. Typical cottages have muted honey-coloured walls of roughly coursed stone, and darker weathered steep stone roofs. A widespread characteristic feature is the dormer window formed by carrying part of the main wall face up above the eaves and finishing it in a miniature gable. Valley junctions between the plane of a main roof and that of a gable roof often were 'swept', that is the stone slates changed direction in a sweeping curve instead of an abrupt angle. The ease with which the stone was worked was celebrated by refined carved details such as mouldings on mullions and lintels. On early and better quality work, in particular, are to be found projecting hood moulds and label stops over door and window openings. Most chimneys were

29

placed in gable walls to serve fireplaces, which, as in other places, became smaller with time.

The visual harmony and popularity of Cotswold cottages such as Arlington Row, Bibury (Gloucestershire), need not be stressed. Bordering the limestone belt are cottages of more mixed building traditions, which have a different appeal. Through geological accident they have complexities which are absent from the Cotswold heartland. What they lack in visual unity to satisfy the eye they make up for in visual diversity to satisfy the powers of reasoning. Stone is mixed with many different bricks and timber, and roofs are thatched and clay-tiled. The intricacies of geographical distribution of the various materials await detailed investigation. In the north of the region the stone, which becomes progressively more brown and orange, is joined by timber and thatch. In the west, beside the Severn, various different stones, including Forest of Dean sandstone, are mixed with brick and clay roof tiles. In the east the Cotswold tradition merges gradually with materials like some in East Anglia. In Berkshire and Buckinghamshire there is a wide range of brick colours from red and brown through grey to blue. Neat shallow arches over doors and windows, and coloured brick patterns are found. In some places, too, are slight timber framing, clunch and wichert.

South-west England

Materials in the south-west are as varied as anywhere and traditions remain less diluted by intrusive later development than in many places. Many of the better quality cottages are in the east of the region, where materials like those in other chalkland areas are found, namely brick, flint, timber, clunch and thatch. Parts of Dorset and Somerset have excellent stone, some of it closely related to Cotswold limestone in appearance and use. Over a wide area south of a line between Exmoor and mid Wiltshire nothing so durable existed, so cob was used. In some villages it is seen at its best, used as the main material and not merely a poor second choice. In such places cob garden walls may be found with thatched 'roofs' like nearby buildings, to keep off the rain which would be so damaging. There is a late eighteenth-century relative of cob, called pisé, which is an unbaked earth and gravel mix made into walls by ramming between temporary timber forms. In the low flat lands around Bridgwater in the late eighteenth century appeared clay pantiles, otherwise a material more typical of the east of England. At the other regional extreme, in the searching climate of upland west Devon and Cornwall, cottages were built of tough intractable stone, such as the granite rubble of Bodmin Moor. Difficulty in working such material led builders to use large uncut blocks,

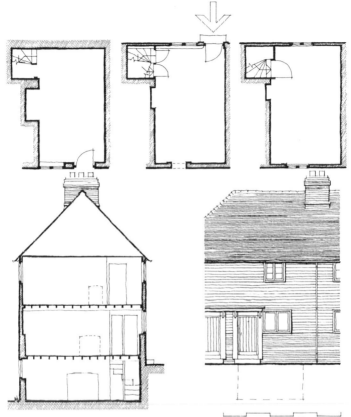

Fig. 18. Late eighteenth-century three-room cottage, Henley-on-Thames (Oxfordshire). Slight timber frame, timber cladding and brick (Upper left) Basement plan. (Upper centre) Ground-floor plan. (Upper right) First-floor plan. (Lower left) Cross section. (Lower right) Front elevation.

which give a massive primitive appearance to older cottages. Some walls on exposed sites were given extra protection by slate hanging in the same local slate as used on some roofs. Life in the far west was hard, so original cottage quality was low and few perishable materials have survived. Even from the other end of the region near Bath there came bleak Georgian descriptions of 'shattered, dirty, inconvenient, miserable hovels, scarcely affording shelter for beasts of the forest'.

31

West central England

Cottages in the region bounded by the Pennines, the Cotswolds and the Welsh hills have suffered less from the climate than many, but more from the later growth of towns. Scattered Georgian industrial villages around Birmingham, the Potteries and other places began to spread and fill in the eighteenth century. Some cottages, like the rows at Coalbrook-dale, have remained untouched by these later developments, and so have ones occupied by remote Shropshire smallholders and Herefordshire farm labourers. The timber tradition was strong and persisted late in the south-west of the region, while varied red-brown brick became the main material in the east and north. Typical cottage appearances are simple and direct, with projecting brick courses known as dentilled brickwork below the eaves, segmental arched window heads of well cut bricks, side-hung timber casement windows with only minimal cills, and glass almost flush with the exterior wall face. In the borders, where coal, clay and transport were least accessible, stone was replaced less by brick. Various red, brown and grey stones were used in other areas, such as parts of north Staffordshire and Cheshire. Roof forms are simple, and commonly finished with plain tiles, but with stone slates in the south-west, heavy stone flags in Cheshire and some thatch in many places. Characteristic chimneys of some earlier cottages are massive at the base and ascend in two or three sharply diminishing stages.

East central England

Mixed large and small farming and early industry gave this region some affinity with the west central region. A central stone-bearing zone running northwards was exploited around Stamford for national and local use. West of the stone, in Nottinghamshire, and east in the coastal half of Lincolnshire, brick was used with a scattering of other materials. Thatch remains and pantiles are common except in the south-west, where there are plain tiles, Collyweston stone and, by 1800, large rough Leicestershire Swithland slates. Lincolnshire fen cottages are like some in Norfolk, with pantiled roofs, wedge-shaped dormers and brick tumbled-in gables. These eastern features merge, perhaps unexpectedly, with the limestone tradition which extends from the Cotswolds and Dorset. To these contrasting traditions was added that of north midland cottage textile industries. This gave brick buildings, some of three storeys, with shallow arched openings and large, many-paned upper-floor windows to provide good lighting by which to work.

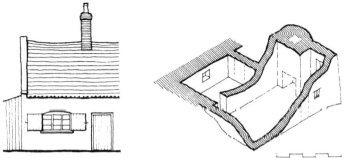

Fig. 19. (Left) Eighteenth-century Fenland cottage, Aby (Lincolnshire). Brick and pantile, one and a half storeys. (Right) Ruined stone cottage with outshut built into hillside, Ffwddog, Grwyne Fawr Valley (Gwent).

Wales

Many Welsh cottages belonged to crofters' holdings scattered thinly over mountain and moor, rather than clustered together as in England. Many of the cottages of early mineral workings also were dispersed and remote and remain so today, some now in ruins. Organic materials have not lasted well in the wet climate and so Wales, perhaps more than anywhere, is now the land of stone cottages. The main exceptions are a very few surviving unbaked earth buildings near western extremities and some timber, mainly near mid and northern borders. A remarkable variety of stone may be seen, including massive boulders and very long thin walling slate in Snowdonia, and sandstone and limestone concealed beneath many coats of whitewash. Much thatch has disappeared, but some early slate roofs survive and are distinguished from later examples by rougher texture and greater thickness. Slate was also used as a floor finish and, as in parts of England, so were pennant flagstones and pitched stone. This consists of pebbles or small flat stones laid on edge to make attractive but uneven geometrical patterns, today confined to outbuildings and yards.

Typical cottages have a simple, unadorned character, which comes from low sturdy forms, plain clipped roofs, stout chimneys and neutral colours. Eighteenth-century travellers were struck by the poor conditions, but today the strongest impression is likely to be of a pleasingly consistent tradition. Early and remotely sited cottages have the steepest roof pitches and small, deep-set openings placed randomly. Many have been enlarged by sideways extension or by raising the roof level, although single-storey buildings are quite common, particularly in the west. Later cottages have symmetrically spaced and taller windows, and sawn and bolted roof timbers instead of rough wooden pegged ones. Early room division by furniture was superseded by timber, stone and occasionally slate slab partitions. A common plan form has a centrally placed entrance leading into a main room with gable wall fireplace. Opening off this at the opposite end were the parlour and a service room. There might be one or two storeys, and sometimes there was a first floor over the parlour only, giving a loft sleeping space reached by ladder from the main room. An alternative was for the entrance to be in a gable wall, where it backed on to the chimney.

North central England

The Pennine range dominates the region although there was some lowland farming, mainly in the east. The principal material used throughout the uplands and some lowlands is stone. Much is sandstone, which was skilfully cut and laid in regular courses, which blackened on exposure. Where neither sandstone nor limestone was used there are bricks, often slightly larger than in the south of England. Pantiles began to replace thatch in the east by the 1780s, but the most characteristic roofs have large heavy stone slabs laid on simple low pitches.

Perhaps more than in other places, specialised buildings for specialised purposes appeared in the Pennines in early industrial times. As well as orthodox cottages for farm labourers, quarrymen and others there are, for example, laithe houses. Many were built for upland West Riding smallholders in the later eighteenth century, although they originated over a century earlier. Each consists of a long block combining separate cottage, byre and barn, which may be identified by a high cart-sized entrance to the laithe. Equally easily identified are cottages for handloom weavers, who reached a peak of prosperity around the end of the eighteenth century. Long ranges of upper windows (some now blocked), with thin stone mullions between, were intended to light the loomshops. A related central Lancashire cottage type had a cotton loomshop either in a cellar or on the ground floor next to the living space. Typical Pennine cottage exteriors are low and sturdy and often adapted to steeply sloping sites. They have plain gables with parapets which terminate at eaves level in stone brackets or kneelers. Windows have plain one-piece upright stone surrounds and mullions set slightly forward of the main wall face. Further east these stern and forthright appearances gave way to lighter ones which recall other east coastal areas.

Northern England

Cottage building north of Lancashire and Yorkshire was

restrained by a hard life enforced by the soil and climate. Farm labourers continued until late to live in farmhouses or outbuildings rather than in separate cottages. Not until the later eighteenth century were permanent materials much used to build the few cottages that were needed. Today, stone walls are found except in the east, where there is brick, and in the north-west, where there is brick and cobble. Roofs are stone flags and a little thatch, with pantiles in the east.

Fig. 20. Upland stone cottage near Marple (Greater Manchester), about 1800

Hard lives were reflected in hard, unyielding stone and archaic cottage forms. Longhouse building continued in Northumberland long after it was abandoned further south. It is probable that small, single-storey cottages made up a larger proportion of the total in this region than elsewhere. In the west Brunskill has noted simple cottages which seem broadly to resemble many in Wales. Single-storey two-room buildings each have a near-central entrance into a larger heated room, off which opens a parlour or bedroom. More common types have one and a half or two storeys, with either one or two rooms on each floor. Among four-room examples wide and narrow frontage versions are found. Roof shapes are simple, without hips and usually without the gable parapets seen not far south. The appearances of today echo the starkness which struck one late eighteenth-century traveller: 'one little piece of glass to admit the beams of day...damp earth...breeze-disturbed embers...disconsolate poultry that mourns upon the rafters...'

4. Georgian polite, 1750-1815

Cottages for aesthetic effect

According to one of George Eliot's characters, the country carpenter Adam Bede, the best designer was 'a practical builder, that's got a bit o' taste'. This was the narrow vernacular view with which many who wanted more than only 'a bit o' taste' would have disagreed. In this chapter are examined polite cottages which were created by the first specialist designers to work on cottages. Widely understood architectural conventions were used in calculated pursuit of aesthetic ends. This gave a cosmopolitan quality which was highly esteemed and absent from the vernacular. Polite cottages were only a minority, but probably a larger proportion of their original number has survived than that of vernacular cottages.

The people who decided to build polite cottages were wealthy, which enabled them to spend more than a bare minimum, and keen to improve their estates. Another distinction was their desire to display improvements and good taste. From the early eighteenth century, major landowners began to landscape the surroundings of their country houses. Emparking, as it is known, went furthest on the prosperous lowlands. New vistas and prospects were opened up, avenues planted, lakes dug and ornamental buildings built. That some of the ornaments could be made to house tenant labourers and gatekeepers was so much the better. What aristocratic landowners did on the grand scale with planned villages, small gentry could imitate at the scale of single cottages. Public undertakings such as turnpike trusts and canal companies, and some pioneering industrialists, also sought respectability by similar architectural means and built polite cottages for employees.

Most occupiers of polite cottages appear to have rented their homes, which were tied to jobs. Probably most avoided the murkiest depths found in the worst crumbling vernacular hovels. Some occupiers such as estate foremen held key positions with matching incomes, and even most of the poorest had a garden, to help keep poverty at bay. In later decades small numbers of impoverished gentry and tradesmen became the first people to occupy cottages out of choice, seeking relief or retirement from the towns. Many found cottages to be a socially acceptable way of stretching a small income to create an agreeable way of life.

A variety of professional architects and enlightened amateurs offered their designs. Enthusiasm, aesthetic sensitivity and good social connections could take the amateur far, and the architects' role and relationship to the business of building was not yet clearly defined. Some designers, like John Nash, were leaders by any standards, to whom cottages were only a minor interest.

Others were authors of architectural pattern books which began to offer designs to all and to introduce country builders to leading ideas.

Formal and informal

There were several origins of polite cottage design. Architectural styles were borrowed from the elevated world of grand architecture, and standards of accommodation roughly resembled those of the better vernacular cottages. Rows of almshouses also had some affinity and maybe sometimes formed part of the ancestry. At first, layouts of cottage groups were systematically planned, but building materials and construction remained more or less purely vernacular. One of the first examples is at Chippenham (Cambridgeshire), where emparking began as early as 1696, under the First Lord of the Admiralty, later Lord Orford. The old village was cleared and replaced by neat pairs of regularly spaced new cottages near to the park gates. The cottages are one and a half storeys high, with colour-washed walls and tiled roofs, each with a dormer. Their siting clearly was the result of deliberation, but their construction owed little to grand architecture. Another very early example appeared in 1729 when Sir Robert Walpole built twenty-five cottages near Houghton Hall (Norfolk). They form a somewhat severe-looking but soundly built brick and pantile group, lining both sides of the approach to the hall. Again, the composition of the group seems to have been regarded as more important than the architecture and construction of individual cottages. A few other examples followed from the 1730s at Thrumpton and Bradmore (Nottinghamshire) and elsewhere. An influential group was built by Lord Harcourt at Nuneham Courtenay (Oxfordshire) from 1761, after the old village had been swept away. Twenty semi-detached cottages were built in two parallel lines along the turnpike road. They are one and a half storey, four-room buildings, built of brick and apparently reused timber framing. Nuneham Courtenay, too, was laid out on a simple plan, but building construction remained vernacular, as in most earlier schemes. These pioneering groups were mainly well spaced, with large gardens, and a clue to their origins is the repetition of similar buildings, rather than solitary isolation or great variety within a group.

Some early designers sought more controlled, closely built urban appearances. One example was Harewood, the Earl of Harewood's village near Leeds, built for workers in a new ribbon factory. The prestigious architect John Carr of York designed it about 1760, with a T-shaped layout of wide streets which aspire to formal grandeur. Variation in the size and height of the stone terraces gives visual interest and once reflected the differing status of occupiers. Another attempt at urban elegance and sense of enclosure appeared at Lowther, near Penrith (Cumbria), about five years later, having been designed by the Adam brothers for Sir James Lowther. Although never finished, the miniature city-like forms of circus and square are complete enough to make an unexpected feature in the remote countryside. Architectural devices of strong symmetry and projecting bays are taken from neo-Classical ideas of composition. The visual effect of the solid-looking stone terraces of one and two storeys is almost as far removed from vernacular informality as could be.

Fig. 21. Milton Abbas (Dorset). Each pair of cottages shared an entrance door.

Lowther is an extreme in grouping because such architectural formality was already falling from fashion when the village was new. In the next few decades the rigidity of some planned groups became more relaxed. This may be seen in the contrast between Lowther and Milton Abbas (Dorset), an estate village begun several years later, in about 1773. Here the rigid straight lines and precise arcs of Lowther were replaced by sinuous curves. Milton Abbas was the work of two leading figures, William Chambers and 'Capability' Brown, who laid out a carefully winding road up a fine valley. Along both sides were spaced forty semi-detached two-storey, four-room cottages, with a tree between each block, and wide grass verges in front. Although the unadorned cottage fronts were traditional, the evenly spaced repetition of the blocks once again betrays the calculating touch of a designer. Milton Abbas replaced an earlier settlement which was a nuisance to the landowner; one man's estate improvement sometimes meant another's upheaval.

Expert contributions

Visual informality made progress among men of taste, such as William Gilpin, who criticised the regularity of Nuneham Courtenay. Uvedale Price also favoured romantic landscapes and helped to spread the idea of the Picturesque. Their views were taken up by designers and patrons, who moulded estates to look like the work of painters who portrayed nostalgic natural scenes. Practical farming began to be hidden behind studied appearances of simple rustic virtues and innocence. Romantic landscapes were enlivened by planned incidents and focal points like the mock castle, folly and rustic cottage. Idyllic scenes were completed with a gentle wisp of smoke rising dreamily among the trees, and happy peasants standing at doors embowered with honeysuckle. By 1780, if not before, all the essential elements of the cottage ideal were present. They remain potent to the present day.

The Picturesque ideal was apparent naturalness and disorder, but the means by which it was created were highly artificial. Uvedale Price listed a whole vocabulary of features for use with Picturesque cottages: they included intricacy, variety and play of outline, asymmetrical positioning of buildings, porches, overhanging eaves, recessed windows and large intricate chimneys. Around and over the cottage there were to be creepers, shrubs and trees. James Malton added to the list in 1798 with irregular breaks in the direction of walls, one point higher than another, and a wide variety of roofing and walling materials. Irregular building forms, harmonious colours and 'smiling verdure' were intended to suggest contented cheerfulness and balance between nature and man. To codify Picturesque elements was almost to caricature the vernacular, but with a key difference: studied deliberation in the Picturesque replaced uninformed spontaneity in the vernacular.

Pattern book designs were more or less influenced by Picturesque ideals. Nathaniel Kent's pioneer book of 1775 suggested a design of unassuming appearance, with square living room, pantry, cellar, bread oven, separate parents' and children's bedrooms and large garden. He thought that separation of boys and girls might be desirable but was too costly and, in any case, boys went away to work at an early age. In most later pattern books the largest number of main rooms was four, which seems to have been at or above the cost limit thought reasonable by most landowners. Designs for smaller cottages were put forward, down to one-room size, although despite this there were attempts to raise standards. Minimum headroom heights

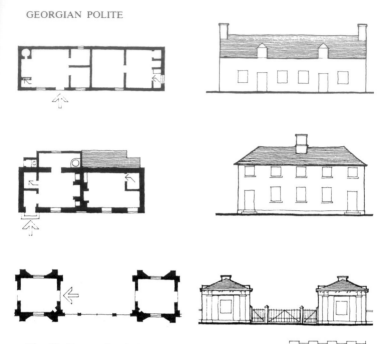

Fig. 22. Pattern book designs. (Upper) Nathaniel Kent, 1775. (Centre) John Wood, 1781. (Lower) Richard Elsam, 1803.

were recommended and there was said to be a need for easy stairs, both features which were common weaknesses in the vernacular. Drier, cleaner ground-floor finishes were suggested and so were tool sheds, privies and more convenient water supplies. John Wood's pattern book laid down principles, intended to avoid the worst existing faults, which today provide insight into enlightened opinion of the time. Dryness and health were to be ensured by raising the ground floor above the surroundings, avoiding building against banks, and avoiding attic bedrooms. All these faults were common vernacular practice and some not unknown in polite cottages. Warmth and comfort would result from walls no thinner than 400 millimetres (16 inches) in stone or 340 millimetres (13½ inches) in brick. Entrances were to be screened and cottages were to face east or south, with carefully positioned doors and windows. An advance on Kent's earlier view was that there should be separate bedrooms for children of each sex. Cottages were to be built in pairs rather than singly, so that neighbours could help one another in times of sickness.

Richard Elsam's *Essay on Rural Architecture* of 1803 shows that many of these principles were not always met, at least by others, even in pattern books. Elsam designed a park entrance keeper's cottage made of two separate single-storey blocks, one on each side of the park gates. On one side was a heated living room with a front door commanding the gates and a back door opposite, opening on to a walled garden. On the other side of the gates, fully 7 metres (22 feet) away, was the bedroom, with the same plan as that of the living room. Perhaps this was a hint that, in practice, one family might occupy each block. The great practical inconvenience of the plan was partly balanced by a carefully designed classical exterior, complete with plinth, pilasters and string course, which would have made a fitting approach to a great country house. The priority given to visual effect above occupiers' convenience was unmistakable.

Bricks and mortar are costly, so it is not surprising that theoretical ideas often ran ahead of what was actually built. Many polite cottages were quite plain and functional with no more than a little decoration. One or two pointed Gothic revival windows or some faintly Tudor hood moulds over openings were often the main evidence that a specialist designer had been at work. Other cottages might lack applied ornament but instead have symmetrical elevations characteristic of many buildings which are drawn and deliberated about before being built. Again, some were built of costly materials such as ashlar stone, matching the great house of the estate. There could be high quality, long lasting and consistent details for stone cills, mullions, window frames and chimneys, made by craftsmen used to working on grand and expensive buildings. These features were uncommon in the more rough and ready approach of vernacular builders, who valued simplicity above regularity and consistency.

An example of this polite though not strikingly stylish way of building is a single storey cottage near Limpley Stoke, Bath, believed to date from about 1810. It had a stone vaulted cellar with four main rooms over, two of which were heated by fireplaces grouped under a central chimney. There is a hipped roof (unlike the local vernacular) and coursed rubble walls with carefully cut stone quoins, lintels, cills and plinth. While some polite cottages were conspicuous by their general form and ornament, this one is conspicuous by close attention to detail. Compared with both vernacular and earlier polite building, the cottage shows general trends in the growth of precision and in avoidance of oversized elements. Wall and roof surfaces are more finely jointed and there are smaller sections of structural timber.

41

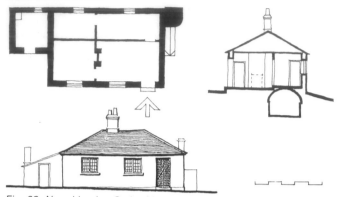

Fig. 23. Near Limpley Stoke (Wiltshire). Four-room cottage with cellar and outshut.

Similar features are present in some cottages built for pioneering industrialists who established colonies in the country-side. Examples are at Belper and Cromford (Derbyshire), where Strutt and Arkwright built some rows of three-storey cottages for their early textile enterprises. They owe much to vernacular practice, but have such polite features as a controlled rhythm of doors and windows on elevation and, in some cases, iron window frames.

Terraces of this sort showed that formal neo-Classical composition, in the spirit of Lowther, persisted despite growing architectural informality in many places. For example, an imposing terrace was built at Elsecar (South Yorkshire) by John Carr in 1799. It consists of a two-storey sandstone rubble block with central and end portions raised to three storeys and projected forward, emphasising the symmetry of the whole. Persistence also of schemes of small, regularly spaced blocks may be seen in a group at East Stratton (Hampshire) designed for Francis Baring in 1806 by the prominent architect George Dance. The cottages have two and a half storeys and are arranged in a line of five semi-detached pairs. Side entrances give access to a front and a back room on each main floor. The wall material is brick on timber framing, with thatched roof and horizontally sliding timber windows, making construction which was close to the vernacular. Here the impression is of generous, practical accommodation using cheap local building skills, rather than concern with visual display. In method and intention not much had changed from the time when Nuneham Courtenay was built over forty years earlier.

Design for turnpike roads and canals was quite different, often with an inventive boldness in the geometry of buildings. A case is the lock keeper's cottage at Pontymoile canal junction (Gwent), believed to date from about 1812. Like many turnpike cottages, it has a prominent convex projecting front which gives good views of approaching traffic. Adjoining the curved-fronted block is a two-storey block of similar size at a lower level on the canal embankment. A partly conical slate roof and large porch add to the strongly modelled white-rendered building form. This example is one of many which were designed to symbolise their purpose and to look different from other cottages not owned by a company or trust.

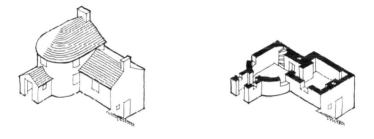

Fig. 24. Pontymoile (Gwent), lock keeper's cottage.

Picturesque progress

Ideas about cottage styles developed and the Picturesque influence continued to grow. Simple rectangular plans were changed to elaborate curved and polygonal ones, with out-houses, porches and canopies. Clusters of great ornamental chimneys sprouted from steep thatched roofs with riots of gables and dormers. Small buildings became loaded with decorative finials, lattice casement windows and fretted barge boards. Some old vernacular cottages were repaired and given Picturesque 'fancy dress' rather than being destroyed and replaced. At times the applied features threatened to overwhelm the underlying building, which was often not large. All this was evidence that an architectural style peculiar to cottages was becoming firmly established. As often happens before the limits to a new idea become apparent, extremes of eccentricity were sometimes reached and passed. One case was at Marford (Clwyd), where George Boscawen built between 1805 and 1816 a series of wilful-looking cottages influenced by the Gothic style. An

43

arresting range of windows was used, of circular, elliptical, lancet and ogee shapes, set in curved walls. Roof planes were built which, even when new, sagged gently downwards near the centre and rose up at gable verges, a notable feature even by Picturesque standards. Such designs easily took on a light-hearted, toylike air, close to frivolity, seldom found elsewhere in British architecture.

Contrast to this whimsicality came from some cottages built to match nearby grand architecture. Various architectural replicas and oddities were occasionally inspired by classical and more remote influences, which were tried out on the houses of the very wealthy. Finely controlled miniature Greek temples with pediments and columns gave balance and crisp lines to some lodges and gatehouses. Examples by one leading architect, Sir John Soane, are the late eighteenth-century classical lodges of polished appearance at Langley Park (Norfolk) and Tyringham (Buckinghamshire). A purpose of such cottages was to reinforce what might be termed the image or corporate identity of an estate; the unity of ownership between great house and cottages was made apparent by linking the architectural style of each.

The Picturesque began to reach superior buildings known as *cottages ornées*, intended for people of means. At poorest the *cottage ornée* was not much better than a labourer's cottage, but at best it approached the size of a villa. Preferably it was to be sited near to a town, where it would be close to society and supplies of provisions. In this, *cottages ornées* may be said to have been a forerunner both of suburban growth and of second homes. These genteel cottages were popularised in the early nineteenth century by building for the Duke of Devonshire and in Windsor Great Park. The architectural aim was to create looks which were 'cheerful and independent' and not in any way poverty stricken. According to Elsam, this required appearance to be 'low, approaching humility', but fully dressed with all the trappings of the Picturesque. One of the peculiarities of fully developed Picturesque was that it could combine modest building structure with extravagant ornament.

Fig. 25. The Picturesque. (Left) Badminton (Avon). (Centre) Lyme Regis (Dorset). (Right) Blaise, near Bristol.

A milestone in the progress of the Picturesque came in 1810 when the first complete Picturesque hamlet was built. It was designed by John Nash for a Quaker banker named Harford in order to house his estate workers at Blaise, near Bristol. A group of ten cottages was arranged irregularly around a gently sloping green, each one different and replete with low eaves, romantic gables and large chimneys. Stone, brick and thatch are combined, using all the Picturesque devices to achieve a studiedly random effect. Typical ground-floor accommodation was a square living room 4.7 by 4.7 metres (15 feet 6 inches by 15 feet 6 inches) with separate spaces for pantry, privy, porch and stairs. A plain man's view today is to ask how much bigger the cottages might have been if money spent on sugary appearance had been redirected to practical ends. This is to miss the point that a main architectural aim at Blaise was to touch the emotions rather than shelter the body. Nash sought to create a sentimental escapist pleasure as much as to provide utilitarian housing units. A hint at what was being escaped from may be seen in the following chapter.

5. Victorian vernacular, 1815-75

A changing society

In the nineteenth century age-old certainties and customs were challenged as industry exerted a powerful though largely remote influence on rural life. In the middle of the century only about half of the population of eighteen million lived in the country, the rural population having grown more slowly than that of the towns. After about 1850 some remote country places began to lose people, and at a quickening rate. The proportion of all working people who were in agriculture slipped from a little over one in three in 1815 to about one in six at mid century. Despite this relative decline there were more farm labourers, almost a million, in the 1850s than before or since. During the early decades after 1815 farming experienced mixed fortunes, and observers such as William Cobbett saw much evidence of hardship, which sometimes led to rick burning. Enclosures were still being made, though more slowly, and efficiency was increasing. Times began to improve gradually from the mid 1830s and more quickly after the repeal of the Corn Laws a decade later. Helped by demand from the towns, the 1850s and 1860s came to be seen as a golden age for farming.

Having been brought low in the Napoleonic Wars, not many farm labourers shared the growing prosperity. Theirs was the worst rewarded major occupation, and it was to remain so long after the prosperous 1850s and 1860s, which brought little relief. The poorest families were those of unskilled casual labourers furthest from the industrial centres. Compared with their hardship, that endured by a minority of skilled men like dairymen, horsemen and wagoners was less. Some households continued to earn a second income from cottage outwork, but new factories continually lessened these opportunities. Instead, more cottagers worked in quarries, rural mines, brickworks and small workshops. Another group, who linked farm and industrial workers, included blacksmiths, carters, cobblers, wheelwrights and others who met the needs of farmers and small manufacturers. Finally, there were various more or less genteel retired tradesmen and others who depended on small investments.

Housing conditions and provision

Evidence that the stock of cottages was too small and in poor condition was not lost on the Victorians. Acute shortage forced families to continue occupying squalid, outworn cottages long after they had been reduced to crumbling mud and thatch. Population growth had overtaken the supply of cottages and led to gross overcrowding, and many families shared their home with cows and pigs. Some cottages seen in 1816 were 'with no other aperture than a door in a mud wall to let out the smoke'. Some animals still remained at the middle of the century and the smoke at least showed that there was enough fuel for a fire. This was not always so, and cottages sometimes went unheated, causing parents, children, grandparents and lodgers to huddle together indiscriminately to keep warm. According to a survey in the 1860s, more than two fifths of cottages had only one bedroom each, and only one in twenty had more than two bedrooms. In nearly all cases ventilation, water supply and waste disposal were still rudimentary. Only after 1850 did growing national wealth begin to offer better prospects to a few. Fortunate families could expect a home with a sound table, chairs, beds, chests, earthenware dishes and even a few ornaments. Much lighting was still by rush lights, with candles for the better-off households. A few began to cook on coal-burning iron ranges instead of open fires.

Some new cottages were provided by speculative builders, who were encouraged by people such as tradesmen and widows looking for outlets 'as safe as houses' in which to invest their capital. Some speculative cottages were cheaply built and only poorly maintained for the same reason as for their scarcity. This was less the result of malice than of wages being too low to allow payment of economic rents. With typical farm wages of about 8 to 12 shillings per week, rent was likely to be only about 1s 6d per week. With cottage building costs in the 1840s ranging from £40 for two rooms up to £100 for four rooms, and an annual rental of £3 to £5, cottages were a poor investment. Allowance for repairs and bad debts made them an even worse one, with far higher returns possible in other fields.

The failure of speculative cottages to meet social need was as tragic for homeless labourers as it was inconvenient for their employers. It followed that many farmers and landowners had no alternative but to provide cottages themselves for their workforces. Some major estate owners built for letting to their tenant farmers, who, in turn, sublet to their labourers. In other cases, freehold farmers built to let directly to their men. Cottages which were tied to jobs in this way could be used as an incentive to attract and keep the most valuable men. Then it might be worthwhile to provide quite good or handsome cottages which belonged to polite rather than vernacular traditions. Much the same applied when someone built a cottage to live in himself. Most owner-occupiers commissioned specialist builders to carry out the work for them, but a few continued literally to build their own houses. In the 1840s mean squatter shelters still could be put up for as little as £10 apiece, although a bigger outlay no doubt helped. Before long, shortage of suitable land restricted the practice of building one's own house and eventually ended it.

Fig. 26. Front elevation, Winster (Derbyshire).

With the death of the do-it-yourself tradition went an opportunity for self-help among the enterprising. The provision of cottages had become more professionalised.

Transition in building

At the beginning of the period vernacular cottages were marked by the local origin of most materials, enforced by high overland transport costs. Materials were used in a near natural state, without much cutting, heating or other processing. Most new work resembled that carried out in the same locality a generation or more earlier. Craftsmen were insular and sceptical of change, the more so furthest from the towns and polite building work. By the end of the period novel and more heavily processed materials were commonly carried longer distances to building sites. The outlook of builders was becoming wider and a little less reliant on custom. Closely connected with these changes was the steep decline of vernacular traditions, which were yielding almost everywhere to universal building methods. Cottages once had differed largely according to place, but now they differed more according to date.

When an innovation arose in cottage building, knowledge of it spread by increased publishing and travel. The railways, more than the canals before them, freed the movement of bricks, tiles, stone, timber and other materials. For the first time cheap bricks

1. Cruck frame, Dymock (Gloucestershire). Painted brick replaces wattle and daub. Thatched roof in course of renewal.

2. Timber jetty and close studding, Lavenham (Suffolk). Market toll cottage, fifteenth century. An early window survives, upper centre. Timbers limewashed in the East Anglian tradition.

3. Wealden house, Cowden (Kent). Later door and brick facing added to front ground floor walls. Timber cladding added to wall nearest camera.

4. Cotswold stone and thatch, Bledington (Gloucestershire). Characteristic stone hood moulds over ground floor windows. Projecting bread oven near camera.

5. Timber box frame, Pembridge (Hereford and Worcester). The frame rests on a stone plinth. Built not later than the seventeenth century. Later raised eaves level revealed by gable wall timbers.

6. East Anglian plastered timber frame, Euston (Suffolk). One and a half storey late seventeenth-century row being re-thatched.

7. Brick and plain tiles, Orford (Suffolk). One and a half storey late eighteenth-century row. Compare the segmental window arches and dormer shape with Euston, plate 6.

8. South-eastern light wall claddings, Groombridge (Kent). Horizontal unpainted timber ground floor walls and plain tile first floor walls. Two and a half storey row built in the eighteenth century.

9. Heavy northern stone window surrounds, Hartington (Derbyshire). Rendered stone cottage of 1777 later subdivided by insertion of right hand central doorway.

10. Plump curves of western cob and thatch, Minehead (Somerset). The plastic material gives wavy lines, small openings and absence of sharp corners. The painted plinth prevents damage by rainwater splash.

11. Georgian polite estate cottages, East Stratton (Hampshire). Two and a half storey semi-detached pair designed by George Dance, about 1806.

12. Gothic picturesque, Marford (Clwyd). Novel ornamental design with circular, lancet and ogee windows, by estate owner George Boscawen, about 1810.

13. Mansard roof, Wormingford (Essex). Brick with timber clad outbuildings and horizontally sliding gable window.

14. *Perishable eastern vernacular, Bramfield (Suffolk). Slight timber framing infilled with mud and covered with lath and plaster. Side-hung casement windows below fixed lights typical of East Anglia.*

15. *One-room upland cottage from Rhostryfan (Gwynedd), now at the Welsh Folk Museum, St Fagans, Cardiff. Massive boulder walls and slate roof, 1762.*

16. Intractable cobble walling, Easington (Humberside). The difficulty of building in this material is shown by partly replaced brick tumbling-in on the gable parapet, and metal straps at the chimney base.

17. *Durable stone and first floor weavers' windows, Heptonstall (West Yorkshire). Stone mullions and the gable kneeler visible at upper right are typical of the strong local stone tradition.*

18. Near-symmetry in brick and slate, Bunbury (Cheshire). The lean-to was probably added after completion of the main block in 1833. Minimal window cills and lower roof pitches were common at that time.

19. Repetitive row of six, Wellers Town, Chiddingstone (Kent). Well built block with ornamental brickwork and horizontally sliding small-paned windows, probably earlier nineteenth century.

20. Neat upright proportions in flint, Blythburgh (Suffolk). Sombre colour of walls brightened by pantiled roof and brick arches and quoins. Datestone 1847.

21. *Universal form, Patrington (Humberside). Narrow frontage pair of 1858, with counterparts in most regions. Elsewhere slate often took the place of pantiles shown here. The vertically sliding sash windows still retain small panes.*

22. Local material in ubiquitous form, Hartington (Derbyshire). Narrow frontage row of 1860 comparable with Patrington, plate 21. The massive stone lintels, cills and gateposts retain local character.

23. Wide frontage, Phocle Green, Ross-on-Wye (Hereford and Worcester). Rubble walls, brick arches, slate roof, side-hung casement windows. When new about 1865, a second chimney existed on the right.

24. Farm building conversion remains, Llanvetherine (Gwent). Two one and a half storey cottages inserted in a barn. Fireplaces on side wall, heavy local stone roof.

25. Romantic Picturesque, Selworthy (Somerset). The work of the estate owner helped by pattern book, about 1828. Picturesque effect helped by thatch, tall chimneys, porch and bread oven. Part of a hamlet which is the property of the National Trust.

26. Developed Picturesque, Ilam (Staffordshire). Estate village design by G. G. Scott, about 1854. Ornamental tiles on walls and roof. Prominent gables and barge boards.

27. *Early eclecticism, Edensor (Derbyshire). Chatsworth Estate cottage, about 1835, with ornament borrowed from a range of architectural sources.*

28. *Simple Victorian polite, Aldford (Cheshire). Stone and slate pair for Westminster Estate, 1856.*

29. *Light embellishment, Compton (West Sussex). Brick and plain tile pair enlivened by ornamental cast iron casements. Compare local materials, including flint garden wall, with Aldford, plate 28.*

30. Private extravaganza, Leigh (Kent). Vertical form contrasts with Darsham, plate 31. Heavily decorated brick and stone to mark a country estate, before 1870.

31. Company cottage, Darsham (Suffolk). Great Eastern Railway crossing keeper's cottage, probably about 1865. Distinctive standard pattern with ornamental brickwork.

32. Arts and Crafts, Buscot, Oxfordshire. Architect Sir Ernest George's interpretation of old Cotswold stone tradition. Estate pair with characteristic stone mullions, roof and gables.

33. Urban forms in the country, Stone (Gloucestershire). Bright red brick and tile contrast with yellow brick quoins and string course; built 1886.

34. Carefully designed revival of early Cotswold style, Eaton Hastings (Oxfordshire). Semi-detached pair built for estate workers, 1893.

35. Revival of west Cotswold vernacular, Painswick (Gloucestershire). Arts and Crafts work by Barnsley Brothers, 1913.

could be bought in places where clay was not available, and Welsh slate found far inland remote from coastal shipping. Some materials producers expanded and undercut their hitherto protected small local rivals. Mechanisation was introduced and handmade goods declined, often unable to compete in price and performance. Some traditional producers of, say, stone slates contrived to continue in business for the time being, but the weakest began to be forced out. Thus, as the railways brought Staffordshire clay tiles into an area, they in effect deprived that area of the use of Cotswold stone slates. The broadening of materials markets from local to regional scale began nearest to large towns and spread deep into the country as secondary railways opened. By 1875 conditions for the survival of the vernacular lingered only in a few remote places. Specialised forms of cottage, like those of handloom weavers, fell victim to much the same forces, when industry changed the ways in which goods were made.

The sweeping extent of change is most obvious in the new dominance of brick over other walling materials. Brick output increased vastly, being helped by the lifting of the brick tax in 1850. After that, mechanisation gradually advanced, at the expense of the old practice of making bricks on the building site. Soft, unevenly fired bricks fell from favour, to be replaced by hard regular shapes of brighter reds, yellows and darker blues. Affinities with site and earth were lessened and there were stronger resemblances to factory products. Greater precision, smoother surfaces and harsher, more strident colours went with bolder wall patterns and sharper, more prominent details around windows and doorways. Many walls were one brick or 225 millimetres (9 inches) thick, with more for good quality work and less for poor. Sometimes external rendering with plaster was used to vary appearances and improve weather protection, but tile hanging and stone, which were comparatively difficult to work, were used less often. One remaining use was in the form of dressed stonework around openings, in decorative contrast to

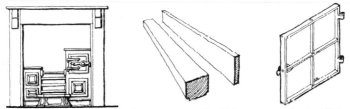

Fig. 27. New materials and components. (Left) Iron range. (Centre) Thin sawn timber joist contrasted with earlier broad-section joist. (Right) Iron window frame.

adjacent brickwork. Another use was in rubble or roughly coursed infill between brick quoins, as decoration or where bricks still cost more. The less durable materials of cob, chalk, clay lump and timber boarding fared badly and were used only in the meanest work. When they decayed they were likely to be replaced with all-conquering brick.

Welsh roofing slate was the other great commercial success which began to penetrate to most places. This dark blue-grey or purple material, of uniform thickness, standard sizes and light weight, benefited from the lifting of tax in 1831. Plain clay tiles and pantiles survived the competition, but heavier and more clumsy roofing materials of limestone, sandstone and Leicester-shire slate declined steeply. Thatch also was rejected more and more, although its cheapness and light weight (on frail walls) sustained it for the time being.

Generally, earlier cottages had been made of variably sized units of great weight and thickness. Later cottages were of more regularly sized units of more precision and smoother texture. By this change weather resistance and durability could be improved, with less deadweight and labour.

There were other losses of local tradition, such as east midland suspended plaster floors. Home grown oak became much more costly than imported pine, and small panes of cloudy and distorting crown glass were replaced by larger ones of superior sheet glass. Earth ground floors gave way to flagstones, bricks, tiles and, for some of the best work, suspended timber joists and boards. New clay chimney pots, coppers for water heating and cast iron fireplaces are reminders that better transport brought cheap household coal as well as brick and tile. Signs that quality was gradually improving through the period included more panelled doors, instead of boarded ones, increasingly fitted with smart Birmingham locks, latches and hinges. Of the many more openable windows, most were side-hung casements, usually timber, but occasionally iron. Superior vertically sliding timber sashes made some progress. The window tax, lifted in 1851, had no bad influence on cottages, since it applied only to larger buildings with more windows.

Plans

There appears to have been more abandonment of plan types which existed by 1815 than emergence of new types. Further studies are needed before a full picture emerges, but it looks as if the earlier decades were the more favourable for experiment, with reduced variety later. Obvious ways in which different types of plan may be distinguished continued to be the number of storeys and the number and arrangement of main rooms. Other differences were connected with numbers and relative positions of fireplaces, stairs, entrances and windows, and the relationships with neighbouring cottages, whether detached, mirror-image attached, or other arrangements. Many cottages continued to appear as hybrids and unique improvisations, so that strict classification is impossible. Six loosely defined groups of plans are outlined, some of which overlap and all of which originated before 1815.

In the first and generally meanest group are single-storey squatter or self-build cottages. Most were improvised from whatever materials could be found and were likely later to be much altered. Generalisations about such frail and inconspicuous buildings are difficult and description of an example must suffice. It stood at Little Dawley, Shropshire, from the 1840s until 1978, when it was re-erected at the Ironbridge Gorge

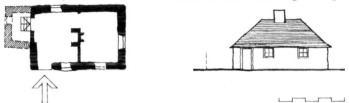

Fig. 28. Squatter cottage, Little Dawley (Shropshire), now re-erected at Ironbridge Gorge Museum.

Museum. As originally built, it had a simple two-room plan which measured 6.4 by 3.8 metres (20 by 12 feet). Sandstone rubble walls enclose a central chimney, and a hipped roof is supported by rough timbers with bark still on them. In 1861 this small cottage was occupied by a married couple and seven children who ranged downwards from twenty-four years of age. Comparable cottages were built elsewhere (some of the 1820s were once recorded at Walton-on-Thames, Surrey) and probably still exist, if only precariously.

The future of farm building conversions, which make up the second group, is equally endangered. They, too, vary widely so that the differences between examples in the same group are sometimes more apparent than the similarities. The group includes a wide range of buildings, the best being workmanlike adaptations with high quality accommodation similar to that of new building. The poorest are makeshift efforts to house an extra farmhand or two through the summer season. At the time of writing an ingenious conversion survives on an isolated upland site at Llanvetherine (Gwent), as ruined evidence of one-time population pressure and later decline. Within an older shell measuring 7.8 by 4.8 metres (25 by 15 feet), which had a highly varied life, two cottages were inserted. Each consists of one large room and one small, on each floor, nested together in two interlocked L plans. The block is one and a half storeys high, with coursed rubble walls, and with some stud partitions (slight timber uprights with plaster on laths) and some stone, ladder stairs and a sandstone roof. The difficulty of making conversions and an idea of living standards are seen in the day-lighting and ventilation provision in the two inner ground-floor rooms. Each has a 'window' which consists only of an aperture measuring 340 by 260 millimetres (13½ by 10 inches) opening on to the adjacent room rather than the open air.

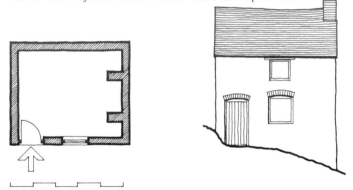

Fig. 29. One up and one down, near Llansantffraid-ym-Mechain (Powys). Original stair position lost.

The third group of plans is made up of small two-storey one-up-and-one-down cottages. At simplest, plans are square or near-square, with door and both windows in the front wall, and fireplace in the gable. This wall and that at the rear are likely to be blank or to have a lean-to outhouse against them. Some of the type are in symmetrical pairs, either with a shared chimney in the central party wall and front doors at far ends of the block, or with doors closer and separate chimneys at each end of the block. Internally there may be the refinements of a pantry, door lobby and staircase lobby partitioned or lightly screened from the main room. Externally the existence of these features may be indicated by small windows. Much or all of the bedroom commonly was in the roof, where principal rafters and tie beams might restrict headroom. The small size of such cottages counted heavily against them and they appeared in shrinking numbers as time passed, probably remaining most common in the poorest districts. Shortcomings of size might be met partly by partition-ing the bedroom, either temporarily or permanently (requiring an extra window), in which case the cottage fell into an

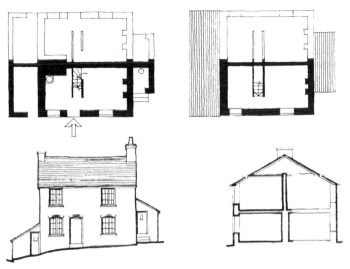

Fig. 30. Wide frontage, Phocle Green, Ross-on-Wye (Hereford and Worcester). This example of about 1865 is unusual in being paired back to back with a mirror-image cottage.

intermediate category with the following group.

The fourth group is made up of wide frontage two-up-and-two-down cottages, which are one of the most typical of the period. They look like a child's image of a cottage, having symmetrical fronts, wider than they are high, with central front door, flanked on each side by two windows, one above the other. The simplest examples have blind gable and rear walls, although those with extra windows, back door and outhouses are more common. The larger of the ground-floor rooms is usually that entered from the front door and is the means of access to the other ground-floor room. Fireplaces may be at one or both gables, and the staircase may either open off the living room (often next to the fireplace) or climb from inside the front door. One bedroom may open from the other, or there may be independent access from a landing. Earlier and poorer examples generally have lowest headrooms, and hence eaves, and smallest, squattest windows. Later and better examples are bigger and taller, with windows to match, perhaps with a third bedroom and a projecting porch. Wide frontage cottages were quite convenient to live in and, having short (front to back) roof spans, simple to build. The group provided accommodation as

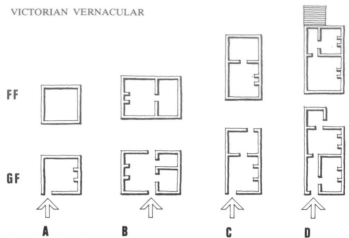

FF

GF

A **B** **C** **D**

Fig. 31. Plans. (Upper row) First floors. (Lower row) Ground floors. A: one up and one down. B: wide frontage. C: simple narrow frontage. D: superior narrow frontage.

good as, or better than, other groups and the best examples of all are more properly houses than cottages.

The other common group is made up of narrow frontage cottages, with the main rooms placed one behind the other, instead of side by side. The front is asymmetrical, with a door on one side and the window to the main room on the other side, and a main bedroom window above. At the rear are a window and a back door to a smaller ground-floor room, and another bedroom window. Small outbuildings are often placed against about half the width of the rear wall, partly enclosing a small yard outside the back door. In superior examples, a third bedroom is fitted in, either at front or rear, or over the ground-floor outhouses. Stairs are placed either across the width of the cottage between front and back rooms, or with a side against a party wall, or winding up in the corner of a room, often next to the fireplace. Simple examples are entered directly into the front room, but other and less draughty ones have a small hall or porch. In superior versions the hall gives direct access to the stairs and the back room, enabling the formal front room to be bypassed if wished. Narrow frontage cottages were well suited for building in pairs or rows and on small sites where narrowness made the best use of available space. Suitability for tight sites was less important in the country than in towns, although narrow frontage types seem to have become more common as time passed. It may be surmised that growing popularity was connected with fashion and a wish to be as up-to-date as the towns. Narrow frontages also had the advantage that they presented to the world a respectable front and banished unsightly domestic scenes to the rear. Accordingly, better quality wall materials and applied ornament are often confined to front elevations. Disadvantages were that it could be darker indoors, because rooms are deeper, and that the wider-span roof was a little less easy to construct.

The final group consists of various less common plans which departed in one way or another from simple rectangular one- and two-storey forms. Included are the usually superior variants of common wide and narrow frontage types, having L- and T-shaped plans. These arose by projecting rooms, or parts of rooms, from the main bulk of the plan to make wings of one or two storeys. Similarly, bay windows and porches might be projected boldly, adding appreciably to the total floor area and creating more interesting elevations and silhouettes. In the same miscellaneous group are cottages which were related to practice in towns, giving three-storey accommodation of three, four or more rooms, apparently more common in the earlier nineteenth century and before, but falling out of use later. A few in the group are 'back-to-earths', with the lowest storey built with one side windowless into the face of a hillside. This type was naturally most common in hilly regions and, like the excavation of cellars, was discouraged by growing concern with damp. Other cottages in the group are some L-shaped plans which nest together in pairs, like the conversion at Llanvetherine. This they might do on plan or in section, or both. No doubt there are other curiosities, which arose from awkward infill sites and builders who did as they pleased.

Taking all groups, a trend over the period is growth in the size and number of rooms of the smallest cottages. Another trend is a

Fig. 32. Narrow frontages. (Left) Baslow (Derbyshire), built of stone. (Right) Potterne (Wiltshire), built in 1849 of brick.

79

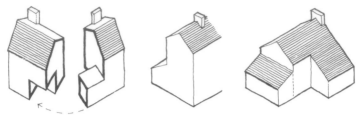

Fig. 33. Complex forms. (Left) Interlock with party floor. (Centre) Three-storey, four-room. (Right) Wide frontage with catslide extension and gable lean-to.

shift from the extremes of long, low masses and narrow, tall three-storey ones towards more compact two-storey narrow frontage forms. Half storeys, or attic bedrooms, were falling from favour, although a small part of the sloping plane of the roof often remained visible in bedrooms with otherwise horizontal ceilings. Windows became larger and front porches were common. Natural and local materials gave way to artificial and universal ones. Appearances evolved towards urban practice, with bigger, more regular buildings in contrast to, rather than in harmony with, their natural surroundings. The rise of universality led to a situation which was not really new. Centuries earlier, there had been a time when nearly all humble buildings, wherever they were built, were made of unbaked earth, timber and thatch. Vernacular diversity was more of a passing phase than a timeless state of affairs. Moreover, new and more standardised ways of building offered compensation for any visual shortcomings by being less prone to repellent insanitariness; there was an overdue improvement in cottage quality. The nature of the better new cottages will be considered next.

6. Victorian polite, 1815-75

Informed opinion

Rural housing and how it might be improved were widely debated in Victorian Britain. Informed public opinion assumed that remedies would come mainly from polite building. Early humanitarian stirrings had begun in the eighteenth century, when prizes were offered for model designs. Concern was redoubled in the 1840s when Edwin Chadwick revealed the unhealthy state of housing in towns. That many cottages were appalling became more and more apparent to those with the will (and stomach) to look. Sanitary and structural defects were bad enough, but even worse was that common decency was often impossible, with both sexes and all ages forced to share bedrooms. Dark hints of cottage depravity shocked tender Victorian susceptibilities. Rural housing took on a moral aspect, partly from heightened public awareness and partly from changing social standards. Cottage improvement societies were founded to show doubting landowners that new cottages could be reasonably economical. It was an uphill task beset by apathy and the sentimental view of an urban nation that the countryside was a harmonious ideal. Even when grim reality was inescapable, there still remained the problem of poor returns on cottage investment. At a mid-century peak in public concern, the best hope for improvement seemed to be a mixture of enlightened self-interest and benevolence by landowners.

Some landowners built actively, but seldom enough to meet needs. Some employers, such as the railways, and a variety of investors and owner-occupiers also helped. The polite cottages which they built early in the period were a minority of the total, but with vernacular decline they became a majority by the end. Many who built polite cottages had motives for doing so which set them apart from their vernacular counterparts. The Georgian aristocracy had already showed that cottages could be a means of creating beauty and displaying ownership and good taste. The more serious Victorian world added the motive of philanthropy. With insurrection thought to be a possibility before the middle of the century, another new motive was to promote social stability. An effect was the use of architectural display to express power and the will to improve the condition of the poor.

Model cottages

Providers of cottages had ample guidance from pattern books and periodicals to help them over the architectural pitfalls of health, morality, style and cost. An idea of the quality of cottages proposed early in the century is seen in Richard Elsam's work of 1816. He suggested that cottages should be sited so as to 'avoid keen blasts of the northern wind'. Sound bricks and stone with good mortar were preferred for walling, for which wood, plaster, mud and clay were much inferior. This enlightened view seems at odds with Elsam's preference for thatch rather than other roofing materials. The main room (which he called the kitchen, but terms varied) should be spacious and ventilated, and the direction and amount of natural light within should be suitable for spinning and knitting. Damp ground floors were to be avoided by laying brick paving, which was cheaper than timber boarding. Space heating by stove was named as a possibility which was economical with fuel, though no doubt costly to install. On balance, Elsam preferred a roomy and comfortable fireplace, which 'in the winter evenings creates social mirth and instructive conversation'. He also believed single-storey buildings to be cheaper than two-storey ones and was in no doubt that more than one bedroom should be provided because of the large families of labourers.

In 1830 Thomas Postans proposed cottages in single-storey pairs, each with living room, two bedrooms, pantry, store, shed and pigsty. Three years later the influential John Loudon wrote his *Encyclopaedia of Cottage, Farm and Villa Architecture and Furniture*. Loudon was a prolific source of model designs in a wide range of types and styles. His interest in gardening as well as architecture came at a time when wider efforts were being made to provide gardens and allotments for hard-pressed labourers. Evidence of rising standards in pattern book designs may be seen in work by J. Young McVicar in 1849. One of his model cottages had an entrance porch, a living room 4.5 by 4.1 metres (14 by 13 feet), a scullery with separate access, sink and boiler, three bedrooms and outside privy and coalhouse. The design was ahead of its time, showing the way towards larger cottages with more bedrooms and services. Such improvements were not inventions of the mid nineteenth century. Their novelty lay in the proposal to provide them for farm workers, as well as their social superiors. Designs for *cottages ornées* continued to appear, although their superior quality made many of them more than cottages in all but name.

Designs of Henry Roberts, published in 1850, were soundly practical, though not lacking ornament or charm. Like Postans, he proposed paired cottages, which were a little cheaper than detached ones. Entrances were at opposite ends of the block, 'to avoid interference between adjoining families', which might otherwise occur, and there was a central chimney. As well as the usual living room, there was a scullery containing a copper, a brick-built oven and a fireplace for summertime cooking, when a fire in the living room was unwanted. The scullery was intended

Fig. 34. Pattern book design. From S. H. Brooks's 'Designs for Cottage and Villa Architecture', about 1832. Impressive appearance but one main bedroom is entirely in the roof.

to be too small to be used as a living room, a practice which Roberts thought undesirable. There were three bedrooms, the minimum which was 'so essential to morality and decency'. At least one bedroom was heated and others without fireplaces had zinc ventilators fitted in partitions. Roberts stressed the importance of secure foundations, southern aspect, good water supply, proper drainage and an adequate garden. The preferred wall material was brick, although stone and flint were possible alternatives. Cob and mud, on the other hand, could not be recommended. Window shutters were assumed to be provided in most cases, but interior plastering was expected only in living rooms. Exteriors were enlivened with fine ornamented chimneys, gables and lattice windows with stone mullions and decorative hood moulds. Large ornamental front-door hinges

Fig. 35. 'Dwellings of the Labouring Classes' by Henry Roberts was the source of this 1850 design.

and handles gave the finishing touch to carefully considered designs. Roberts's grasp of detail was noteworthy for, where garden lavatories were too prominent, he went to extraordinary lengths to disguise them: 'the appearance of a pile or stack of fuel wood is given by a casing of split or half-round larch timbers laid horizontally . . . interior framing may be bricknogged and the roof a slab of slate or strong zinc.'

A quarter of a century after Roberts's ideas were published many designs were little changed, although if anything plainer in appearance. One narrow frontage example by James Simon and Francis Miller had a small front hall which contained the stairs and gave access to a front room. The kitchen (which Roberts would have called the scullery) was also reached off the hall and contained a sink and copper for water heating. A pantry opened off the kitchen, and an adjoining outhouse water closet and coalshed were approached out of doors at the back. There were three bedrooms on the upper floor of this quite large and very well serviced design. Outside, the prominent central chimney, gable and lattice casements gave a typically somewhat Tudor look which recalled Roberts's designs. Other characteristic features of later work were details like robust heavy doorsteps and window cills, iron pipework for rainwater disposal and stout internal joinery fittings of dresser, cupboards and newel stairs. The solidity of such fittings has seldom been surpassed in British low cost housing.

Built examples

What was built was influenced by but did not always match pattern book designs. The most architecturally ambitious built cottages usually showed the influence of the Picturesque. An early example stands at Selworthy (Somerset), in a fine steep narrow valley. The Picturesque potential of the place was recognised by the tenth Baronet Holnicote when he set out to house some estate pensioners in 1828. Cottages grouped with carefully considered informality around a sloping green recall the earlier Blaise, but Selworthy differs in building materials and the origins of the design. Materials were intended to resemble the local vernacular, with thatched roofs and an appearance of cob walls. There are the usual Picturesque devices of tall chimneys, some with projecting bread ovens, eaves swept low, and many gables and dormers. An effect of domesticity is heightened by such details as lattice casements, wicket gates and rustic timber posts supporting canopies. Selworthy was the work of an enlightened amateur, the Baronet himself, probably guided by P. F. Robinson's pattern book *Rural Architecture*. Original enthusiasm for the Picturesque stretched as far as providing Selworthy cottagers with scarlet cloaks to wear about the hamlet.

Picturesque ideas flourished widely, perhaps most notably at Ilam (Staffordshire), Old Warden (Bedfordshire) and Somerleyton (Suffolk). In each case a wealthy landowner created a small settlement of romantic-looking cottages to embellish his estate and house people who worked on it. All three examples

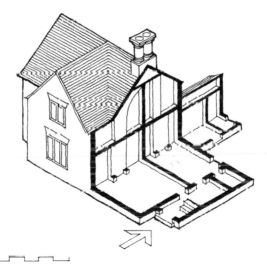

Fig. 36. £250 was the estimated cost of a pair by Simon and Miller in 'House-Owner's Estimator' of 1875.

date from around mid century, when Picturesque influence was at its height. Later decades brought slow decline, but not before the Picturesque had inspired many villages, hamlets and single cottages. Where the influence was strongest there were great clusters of barley-sugar twist chimney shafts with exaggerated cappings, towering above steeply pitched roofs with low eaves. Walls of varied texture and colour were irregularly punctured by pointed Gothic arches and small, oddly shaped casements, often divided into equally oddly shaped panes of glass. Buildings with such features represent one of the peaks of cottage architecture. No other cottages, in such numbers, attained such distinctive appearances and so strongly embodied the essence of cottage character. Plenty of others were as charming to look at and more conveniently planned, but the forms of most were derived from other buildings, as much as being conceived as cottages in their own right.

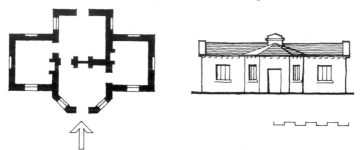

Fig. 37. Toll cottage designed by Telford, 1829, as re-erected at Ironbridge Gorge Museum.

At the same time as the Picturesque developed into a sort of cottage apotheosis, other architectural ideas also were pursued. In particular, Classical ideas were used which reflected the styles of some major buildings. When grand Classical houses were built, the associated ornamental cottages could be made to match, as in the eighteenth century. The following example shows that the Classical influence sometimes extended beyond the vicinity of large houses. The engineer Thomas Telford built about half a dozen tollhouse cottages along his improved Holyhead road in 1829. Today the one formerly at Shelton, near Shrewsbury, stands re-erected in the Ironbridge Gorge Museum. At the front of the brick single-storey cruciform plan, in a central projecting bay, is the 3.8 by 3.8 metre (12 by 12 foot) main room with front door and windows overlooking the road. Behind is a kitchen of the same size and on either side are the two slightly smaller bedrooms. Classical influence is seen in the symmetry of the plan, with prominent central projecting entrance, emphasised by a canopy on columns, and wings on both sides. Symmetry and formality are reinforced by carefully positioned windows and shallow ornamental recesses, like blocked windows, placed centrally in certain walls. Symmetry is strengthened by the flues, which are gathered into one chimney in the centre of the building. The low pitched slate roof also emphasises the Classical appearance in sharp contrast to, say, the steeply jumbled Picturesque roofs at Selworthy. Shelton and other Classical cottages are as controlled and regular as Picturesque ones are informal and relaxed.

Shelton, Selworthy and similar cottages are extremes in being so arresting in appearance. Cottages as eye-catching as these were always a minority, most of which were built at the hearts of estates. The next few examples are more typical in being designed for economy rather than for architectural showmanship. Many were built on estates, but on less prominent sites at a distance from their great houses. The large Holkham Estate (Norfolk), had an extensive programme of building quite simple cottages. Pairs of Holkham cottages of 1819 each had a living room 5.4 by 3.8 metres (17 by 12 feet), off which opened stairs, a back kitchen 4.1 by 2.9 metres (13 by 9 feet) and a small pantry. Upstairs there were two bedrooms at the front and a long, low bedroom at the rear. In the garden there was a separate block containing a wash house, privy and pigsty. The straightforward appearance came from a hipped roof, central chimney and lack of ornaments other than a simple plinth, string course and datestone. Detail plan changes made in cottages built a year later were the removal of the staircase intrusion into the living room and the narrowing of the frontage. This reduction in an already narrow frontage plan was compensated for by an increase in depth, which made a slightly more economical cottage shell without loss of space. There was a further move in 1831 towards narrower frontages, making semi-detached blocks more nearly square on plan. By then the hipped roof was giving way to gable roofs embellished at the front with small gable windows. In the mid 1850s and 1860s higher eaves (indicating higher headrooms within) and entrance porches appeared. At that date Holkham cottages seem, on average, to have been no larger than they were two or three decades earlier. Nevertheless, by the 1860s they cost Lord Leicester about £100 or more each, compared with only about £60 in 1790.

The Duke of Bedford's estate cottages in villages such as Willington and Woburn (Bedfordshire) were regarded when new as exemplary in quality and number. They had two main ground-floor rooms, either two or three bedrooms, brick walls and fairly plain appearances. Another owner of a large estate active in building was Lord Wantage, who set up a brickworks and yard, blacksmith's shop and steam-powered machinery. After clearing away inconvenient 'farm sheds, muck yards and hovels' Lord and Lady Wantage built a series of brick cottages at Ardington and Lockinge (Oxfordshire). Those of the 1860s were quite large, having living rooms 4.8 by 4.8 metres (15 by 15 feet), kitchens and three bedrooms. In each large garden were a coal store, an earth closet and an outhouse containing a copper. Steep roofs, tall chimneys, decorative windows and porches in the Gothic revival style convey an effect of balance between Picturesque frivolity and the practical requirements of everyday life. Comparable estate cottages were built wherever large landowners made improvements. Ornamental datestones are an identifying feature, many with the owner's coat of arms or initials.

Fig. 38. Estate cottages. (Left) Lockinge (Oxfordshire) for Lord Wantage. (Right) Willington (Bedfordshire), 1849, for the Duke of Bedford.

Eclecticism

As the Picturesque slowly waned from the 1860s, it was absorbed into a broad romantic view about ideal cottage appearances. Loosely defined Picturesque ideas for whole landscapes became overshadowed. In their place were more explicit ideas for reviving architectural styles. A whole range of these was put forward from early in the century, including what were called mock-Tudor, Italianate Renaissance, Swiss Chalet, Old English, Castellated Gothic, Monastic Gothic and even Indian Gothic. Revivals and inventions in such styles were used to create effects which were loosely related to the now diluted Picturesque. This eclectic approach was to be expected, since a keynote of much major Victorian architecture was free borrowing from various historical sources. Loudon and many others put before a receptive public all kinds of styles adapted for cottages.

Different styles could be interchanged at will in order to dress up basic plans to suit the preference of the owner. Such borrowing of past styles may be seen well in the Chatsworth Estate village of Edensor (Derbyshire), begun in 1838 by Joseph Paxton and John Robertson. Few places show such wholehearted commitment to eclecticism as Edensor, which is an extreme, with styles ranging from 'sturdy Norman to the sprightly Italian'. More often, borrowed styles were applied only to a cottage or two, and also watered down in appearance. Scattered examples may be found which were built for landowners, parish schools and railway companies like the Midland. It seems that later in the period looks began to owe more to utility and less to style. The change partly reflected a shift among providers of cottages, as Georgian aristocratic individualism yielded to the more businesslike approach of wealthy Victorians and their new institutions.

Effort which had formerly been put into the likes of rustic canopies and mock arrow slits was redirected to more functional ends. As aesthetic gestures became weaker, they were compensated for by bigger, more convenient cottages, which were less damp and better heated, ventilated and lit. Most of the new standards and ideas came from practices first developed in the towns. During the earlier emergence of the Picturesque, leading ideas about cottage design had grown from cottages themselves. Now, new developments depended more upon ideas borrowed from other fields elsewhere; the source of change was alien rather than from within.

By the 1870s the heroic age of cottage building was passing. Numerically, as well as architecturally, activity and interest were moving from the countryside. Vernacular traditions had all but merged with polite, and rural building methods were coming to resemble urban ones. Typical cottages (if such can be said to have existed) were taking on a dilute Tudor appearance with strong practical undertones. Simple cottage shells were provided, to which were added a few ornaments of vaguely historical origins. The dominance of external appearance for onlookers over internal convenience for occupiers was fading. There were three component parts to the emerging style: vernacular remnants, or what cottages had once been; echoes of the Picturesque and historical revivals, or what cottages should be; and urban novelties, or what cottages were becoming.

7. Late cottages, 1875-1914

Rural decline

In the last quarter of the nineteenth century the movement of people from the countryside accelerated from trickle to flood. By 1900 only one in every five people still lived there, 100,000 labourers were leaving the farms every decade, and the 'flight from the land' was a public issue. Underlying the decay was agricultural decline, which followed loss of markets due to cheap food imports. With the passing of prosperous high farming, land went out of cultivation, cottage building diminished and dilapidation was unchecked. Amid the gloom one ray of hope was that the movement of families from the country helped to reduce overcrowding. Another was that there was a tentative start with legislation intended to make new cottages healthier. Again, growing scarcity of labourers began to raise their wages, despite the disaster facing many farmers. By about 1900 the worst times were over. One small sign of this was the candid remark of a cottager in 1902 that 'We've got very partickler about smells now...'

A small but growing number of cottagers were people who moved against the prevailing trend and migrated from the towns for pleasure. In a wealthier and more populous Britain than ever before, more people were able to choose where to live, instead of accepting where they were born. They were helped to do so by better public transport and, in Edwardian times, private cars. In 1913 Lawrence Weaver wrote in *The 'Country Life' Book of Cottages Costing from £150 to £600* about cottagers who were 'the clerk who lives outside the town, the "week-ender" or the people of moderate means and refined taste whose permanent home must be built with severe regard to economy'. The towns which had sapped so much rural life now gave some vitality in exchange.

Reformers and providers

Rural housing issues were hard-headed economic, social and sanitary ones, rather than those of appearance and pleasure. Indeed, it was possible to see a conflict between aesthetic and practical requirements. One writer condemned the Picturesque, which, he asserted, made inhabitants suffer. He said there was a 'picturesque cruelty by every inch of height and light and air of which [sloping roofs and tiny windows] deprive human beings'. This recognisably modern view concerned with effects on the health and pocket far more than on the eye and emotions found growing support. Attempts to improve matters by legislation effectively began with the 1890 Public Health Amendment Act. This had an uneven influence on new cottages, and difficulty arose when some authorities enforced inappropriate urban standards upon unwilling rural builders. At first, control of space, light, ventilation, structural soundness, waste disposal and damp did not go far. It did nothing to ease the shortage of cottages, but worsened it by discouraging builders with the threat of higher costs. By the early Edwardian period cottage building had fallen to a very low level. Because agriculture was weak and investment in cottages unprofitable it seemed that the only hope for rural house building might lie with local authorities. But all action was halted by the war in 1914.

The older aesthetic view of cottages survived alongside that of the politicians and sanitary inspectors. This view was in the tradition of the Picturesque, based on the romantic myth of past bucolic contentment. At a glance cottages looked reassuringly constant, when all about them was in flux; for those who looked closely, there was poignancy in the decay of tradition. Then, as now, nothing compelled affection in a building so much as the possibility of its loss. As it became more difficult to build cottages traditionally, or even to build them at all, their appeal grew. While their reality crumbled into the ground, so the images of cottages were recorded. Painters such as Helen Allingham and Myles Birket Foster added their impressions to those of authors and photographers like Guy Dawber and W. Galsworthy Davie. There was growing interest in preserving cottages, partly because of the influence of the Society for the Protection of Ancient Buildings (SPAB). Ways in which to improve old cottages without spoiling them were shown by C. R. Ashbee and others. What the practical men would destroy in order to start again, the aesthetes tried to adapt and preserve, or at least remember.

Probably a growing proportion of the small output of cottages was the work of professional architects, including such gifted men as Edwin Lutyens and Clough Williams-Ellis. A few wealthy clients wanted ornamental cottages and others looked for experiments by which to house employees at low cost. Once or twice there was a competition intended to arouse interest in new building methods, as in 1905 at Letchworth. Even in more mundane cases, architects were more likely to be employed than before, partly because of bylaw requirements. In districts where there was official control, the old casual approach to building with few or no drawings was discouraged. Under the bylaws, drawings had to be submitted in advance for approval, lessening scope for spontaneous on-site improvisation.

Fabric and form

Building materials from local sources, fashioned on site, continued the retreat begun several generations earlier. Materials such as new cob walling declined from rarity to near extinction, and machine-made joinery arrived from the towns and overseas. Bylaws discouraged some traditional materials, like earth floors and thatched roofs, for reasons of health and fire risk. Among the many materials which disappeared were Devon slates and, in 1909, Cotswold roofing slates from Stonesfield (Oxfordshire). The use of Welsh slate reached a peak about 1900 and stone continued to be replaced by brick. Occasionally there appeared cavity walls made of two leaves of brickwork separated by an air gap, and more interior walls were finished with plaster instead of limewash.

New branded building goods like decorative roof ridge tiles, chimney pots, copings and plumbing parts spread from the towns and suburbs where they first appeared. Several substitutes for major traditional materials were tried out, such as coloured asbestos-cement slates, concrete roof tiles and mass concrete walling. Another novelty of which traces probably survive was the prefabricated cottage. It was shipped in pieces direct from works to site, for rapid assembly on a prepared base. Examples advertised in the 1890s by Messrs Harbrow of Bermondsey included sheet corrugated iron huts for shepherds and keepers, as well as cottages. By 1912 they offered timber-framed bungalows ('Design no. 139a') for £280, but traditional builders withstood the competition. A different approach was that of some architects who tried to revive obsolete wall materials such as clay lump, chalk and timber cladding. In doing so they were reacting to the appearance of ubiquitous brick and slate and trying to keep down costs. The attempted revival of old ways of building was connected with growing appreciation of old cottages by a sophisticated minority.

The range of plan types continued to present a great variety, of which the two-storey majority again may be divided crudely into those with narrow frontages and those with wide. It appears that wide frontages were preferred by enlightened opinion, and where resources were greatest. They were the type usually chosen for ornamental and high quality cottages. Equally, it seems that narrow frontages were preferred for the more functional and plain cottages. For a cottage of a given floor area, the narrow frontage presented a less generous appearance to the world, although it might make up a little in height what it lacked in width. In rows of two or more, narrow frontage cottages needed less external wall for a given floor area than wide frontage ones, hence they could be cheaper to build. Some narrow frontage cottages were the same as large numbers built in the towns. These urban fragments, set incongruously in rural places, showed that some country cottages had lost their separate identity.

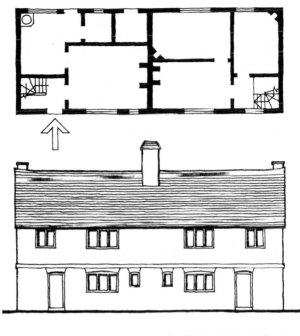

Fig. 39. Wide frontage pair, Brandsby (North Yorkshire), 1905.

The faintly Gothic or Tudor appearance which evolved earlier in the century continued to be built, with steep roofs, large chimneys, lattice windows, gables and porches. Coloured brickwork wall patterns and, particularly later, plaster exterior finishes were used and exposed timber framing was revived, but it was often thin and ornamental rather than structural. There were larger cottages having more complicated floor plans with bays and projecting wings, which gave rise to equally complicated roofs with gables and valleys. Some pairs of cottages were arranged in L form on plan, with one cottage turned through a right angle, relative to its neighbour. Superior cottages had more decorative brickwork, fretted barge boards, porches and three-sided bay windows, as in towns. In detached, semi-detached and end-of-terrace examples, extra windows and extensions could be provided at the gable walls. Where money was scarce and visual interest not much looked for, short straight rows of three or four

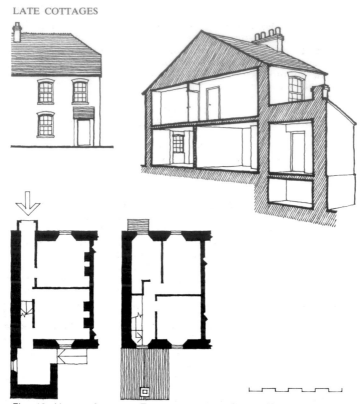

Fig. 40. Narrow frontage, Tregavarras, near Gorran (Cornwall), about 1880.

cottages were more likely. With change in major architectural fashions and less money generally available, the simplest cottages were plain brick and slate boxes. Ornament was limited to carved lintels or arches in a colour which contrasted with that of the walls. Large stone window cills, heavier than before, became common and so did vertically sliding sash windows. Severe outlines were softened slightly by lean-to sculleries and outhouses at the rear, and by robust garden walls, stout gateposts and steps.

Cottages of the same size as the smallest built in the first half of the nineteenth century virtually ceased to appear. Typical accommodation now consisted of a living room (or kitchen), where food was cooked and eaten; a scullery, where washing and other household tasks were carried out; a larder; and three bedrooms. Sometimes there were only two bedrooms, but it seems this was no longer so in most cases. Fourth bedrooms and parlours remained rare in labourers' cottages, although they were within reach of better-off households. Most stairs linked separate hall and landing, rather than being in the living room or bedroom.

Building services advanced but remained backward by urban standards. Old problems of energy supply were met by widespread use of coal for cooking and heating. Unheated bedrooms became less common and kitchen ranges with ovens were recommended, if not always afforded. A bath was of questionable value on grounds of space and cost and 'because it is apt to be used for any other purposes than bathing'. Electric lighting was confined to the houses of the wealthy, and gas lighting was far more a feature of town than country, so cottagers made do with candles and oil lamps. Water supply and waste disposal progressed, but reliable public services had far to go. Water continued to be drawn from private wells, springs and rainwater butts. Water closets were prone to problems due to insufficient water and drainage defects which might contaminate drinking water supplies. Earth closets were free of most of these difficulties and were favoured for country districts. Interiors gathered varieties of pipes, and back gardens increasingly filled with outbuildings. With wash house, lavatory, pigsty and stores for fuel, tools and garden, these amounted in mass to a minor wing of the cottage. Rising standards of living allowed gardens to lose some of the look of bleak vegetable patches and to gather decorative flowers and shrubs.

Alterations to old cottages were often preferred to building afresh, because they were more simple. A common improvement was to combine three old cottages into two, which reflected a general trend towards larger floor areas and more rooms. Another improvement was to lift the level of the roof, or at least the eaves, when replacing the roof finish, which reflected a trend towards higher headrooms. Further improvements were to enlarge windows and to add new outbuildings and porches, which reflected trends towards better daylighting, ventilation, services and, again, more space.

The flow of architectural ideas was not entirely one way, from town to country. Some later architects looked to the country for inspiration, partly to escape the monotony of endless urban terraces. The best of the Arts and Crafts movement, mostly in large houses, but some at cottage scale, became the admiration of the world from the 1890s. The work of architects such as Baillie Scott, Gimson, Lethaby and Voysey left its mark on cottages designed by others. Again, reformers such as Ebenezer

Fig. 41. Design by A. H. Clough, about 1905, for £130 in south-east England.

Howard began to try to combine the advantages of life in the country and life in the town in ambitious new garden cities and garden suburbs. The few cottages in these early twentieth-century planning experiments had an influence on small numbers elsewhere. Such cottages showed a rejection of narrow frontages, long unbroken rows and the old, unhealthy practice of packing many buildings closely together. Instead, there were short blocks of wide frontage cottages with good front and rear gardens, and ample space all around them. Designers aimed at good daylight, sunlight, ventilation and health for the occupiers, and they tried to avoid monotony. Arbitrary and costly ornaments were regarded as wasteful, and materials were chosen with great care for their subtlety of colour and texture. Many of the resulting cottages were light, bright, simple and inventive. They had clean, cheery-looking, light-coloured external walls and clay-tiled roofs, in contrast to the strident red brick and oppressive purple slate of the towns. Mansard roofs, dormers and gables were often used in order to avoid box-like appearances, which threatened where ornaments were few.

By the later part of the period the old distinction between vernacular and polite cottages had disappeared. It was replaced by a distinction between what may be called polite functional cottages and polite ornamental ones. The key now was whether a cottage was built only to satisfy simple functional needs, or also to look good. Ornamental cottages, always a minority, appear to have fallen to an even smaller proportion of the total being built. Most of the remaining new cottages were unassuming and simple, if not severe.

The significance of late ornamental cottages was less in numbers than in influence on subsequent events. This was only to be seen years later in the heavy building which followed the First World War. Then vast new 'cottage estates' of local authority houses arose, together with ribbons and suburbs of private speculative houses. These were the successors which carried forward some cottage traditions. Many compact, manageable and independent dwellings with small gardens, mock oak beams, gables and stained glass had strong cottage associations. Country cottage building never revived after 1914, but the romantic myths surrounding it were an enduring source of ideas. They were ideas about the nature, place and look of a good life within reach of all.

8. Rarity recorded

The prospect for cottages is bittersweet: appreciated, but threatened by decay, neglect and misplaced attempts at improvement. As comfort and convenience are exchanged for authenticity, and as rarity grows, so survivors become more highly esteemed. There has long been anxiety about their future. Rapid destruction was deplored in the 1930s, as it was in the 1890s. As early as 1798 cottages were said to be 'fast falling away, and succeeded by others possessing not a single quality gratifying to the mind or sight'. Every modern age has had its fears, yet with the passing of one generation of cottages another has been found to take its place. This has occurred by change in public taste rather than by new building. Whether it will continue, with no longer any separate tradition of new cottage architecture, remains to be seen.

Fig. 42. Before and after. (Left) As built. (Right) After insensitive modernisation.

The task facing the enthusiast is to record survivors, particularly those threatened with demolition and alteration. Unusual cottages and those typical of once common practice deserve equal attention. The simplest record is a bare outline in photographs and notes. Full exterior photographic coverage will be more useful than this, with some measured overall dimensions and notes about materials and construction. Better still will be to add a sketch plan showing room sizes, wall thicknesses and positions of stairs, windows, fireplaces and other features. The ideal record will consist of accurately scaled plans of all floors, all elevations and a cross section, with photographs and notes. In a few cases there may be archaeological investigation of wall surfaces and roof structures concealed by plaster, and excavation below ground.

Surveying and recording needs only simple equipment, a systematic approach, patience and the owner's permission. The equipment consists of notepad, pencil, camera and tape (30

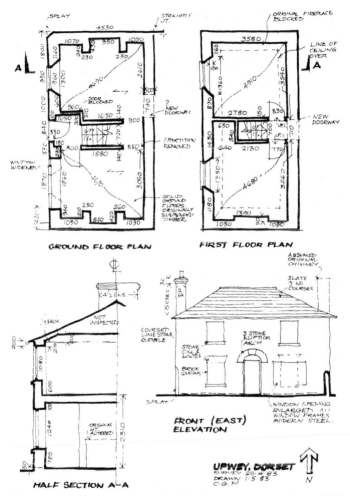

Fig. 43. Part of survey notes of wide frontage cottage, about 1860.

metres linen is best, but 3 metres steel retractable will be enough for many tasks). Surveys may be carried out alone, but groups of up to three will do it quicker, if aims and methods are agreed. Surveyors first should familiarise themselves with the cottage and setting, searching for evidence of alterations and additions, such as straight joints in walls. Second, freehand plans, elevations and section are drawn and, third, measurements are taken. Move in a clockwise direction systematically round every room, and include diagonal dimensions to establish plan squareness. 'Running' dimensions, from a single origin, will avoid cumulative errors in long runs of dimensions. Plans should be treated as horizontal sections, taken at about waist height, although liberties may be taken to include for example, high level windows. Overhead details, such as beams, may be shown in a broken line on the plan. Cross sections should be positioned to show as much useful information as possible, including roof height, stairs and windows. Elevations customarily show the floor level as well as the unreliably variable ground outside. When estimating inaccessible chimney and gable heights, it may be useful to note that brick courses rise by consistent dimensions often measurable near the ground. The best way to proceed is by trial and error, starting with a simple building.

The fourth step is to draw up the survey to scale, preferably while the memory is still fresh, although to wait for photographs may help. A small drawing board, tee-square, adjustable set square, pair of compasses, H or 2H pencil, eraser and draughting pen will be needed, as will a scale rule with 1:100 and 1:50 scales. Begin by drawing the ground-floor plan on tracing paper, which will accept erasures and allow successive plans to be superimposed. Compasses should be used to strike intersecting arcs which will locate the corners of rooms by means of triangulation. Dimensional discrepancies are almost certain to arise and, if large, another site visit will be needed. If small, say, of the order of 25 millimetres (1 inch), they need not be regarded as important. At worst, some timber-framed buildings are neither truly straight, upright, square nor level!

Experience will enable drawings to be related to one another on the sheet, so as to simplify drawing. For example, sections may be placed alongside elevations, with vertical dimensions transferred from one to the other by light horizontal lines. Sometimes, axonometric and exploded views may be used to convey much information with little drawing. The finished drawing should be inked in, possibly freehand rather than ruled if the irregularity of the cottage suggests it. The aim is to communicate accurately without superfluous lines, so nothing should be drawn which is not known to exist, nor anything left off which may help interpretation. The drawing should be completed with neat annotation and title, including identity, date and scale. Black and white photographs are more useful than colour transparencies (except for lecturing purposes), because they last well and are easily copied and enlarged. True elevational photographic views are ideal, because they minimise distortion due to perspective. Details such as window openings, fireplaces and roof timbers are often worth photographing. The information value of photographs is greatly increased by inclusion of a scale rod or other object so that sizes may be gauged.

The next step beyond a record is a study which throws light on how and why a cottage was built and occupied. Documentary sources include title deeds, directories, probate inventories and census enumerators' returns. There are also tithe redemption maps, early Ordnance Survey maps and estate maps. The places to look are the local collections of libraries, museums and county record offices. Questions about occupiers, builders and fabric are ones which help to bring a study alive and, ultimately, to save cottages for others to enjoy. This goal will be brought nearer if the study is made widely available by being deposited with a museum and local history society.

Places to visit

Good places to start are the well-known 'showpiece' villages to be found in tourist guides and in J. Hadfield, *The Shell Book of English Villages* (Michael Joseph, 1980). Planned villages are noted in G. Darley, *Villages of Vision*. Less evident, and often further off the beaten track, something of interest exists in almost all rural areas. Access to some cottage interiors, explanation and publications will be found at the following open air museums:

Avoncroft Museum of Historic Buildings, Stoke Heath, Bromsgrove, Worcestershire B60 4JR. Telephone: 01527 831363.
Chiltern Open Air Museum, Newland Park, Gorelands Lane, Chalfont St Giles, Buckinghamshire HP8 4AD. Telephone: 01494 871117.
Ironbridge Gorge Museum, Wharfage, Ironbridge, Telford, Shropshire TF8 7AW. Telephone: 01952 433373.
Museum of Welsh Life, St Fagans, Cardiff CF5 6XB. Telephone: 01222 569441.
Weald and Downland Open Air Museum, Singleton, Chichester, West Sussex PO18 0EU. Telephone: 01243 811348 or 811363.

Further reading

Ayres, J. *The Shell Book of the Home in Britain*. Faber, 1981.

Barley, M. W. *The English Farmhouse and Cottage*. Sutton, 1987.

Barley, M. W. *Houses and History*. Faber, 1986.

Brown, R. J. *The English Country Cottage*. Robert Hale, 1979.

Brunskill, R. W. *Illustrated Handbook of Vernacular Architecture*. Faber, 1987.

Brunskill, R. W. *Traditional Buildings of Britain*. Gollancz, 1985.

Brunskill, R. W. *Vernacular Architecture of the Lake Counties*. Faber, 1978.

Burnett, J. *Social History of Housing 1815-1985*. Methuen, 1986.

Caffyn, L. *Workers' Housing in West Yorkshire 1750-1920*. HMSO, 1985.

Cave, L. F. *The Smaller English House*. Robert Hale, 1981.

Clifton-Taylor, A. *The Pattern of English Building*. Faber, 1987.

Cook, O. *English Cottages and Farmhouses*. Thames & Hudson, 1985.

Cunnington, P. *How Old is Your House?* Black, 1988.

Darley, G. *Villages of Vision*. Paladin, 1978.

Harris, R. *Discovering Timber-Framed Buildings*. Shire, third edition 1993; reprinted 1995.

Harrison, B., and Hutton, B. *Vernacular Houses in North Yorkshire and Cleveland*. John Donald, 1984.

Iredale, D., and Barrett, J. *Discovering Your Old House*. Shire, third edition 1991; reprinted 1994.

Lander, H., and Rauter, P. *English Cottage Interiors*. Weidenfeld & Nicolson, 1989.

Lowe, J. B. *Welsh Country Workers' Housing 1775-1875*. National Museum of Wales, 1985.

Lyall, S. *Dream Cottages*. Robert Hale, 1988.

McCann, J. *Clay and Cob Buildings*. Shire, second edition 1995.

Machin, B. *Rural Housing: An Historical Approach*. The Historical Association, 1994.

Mercer, E. *English Vernacular Houses*. HMSO, 1975.

Penoyre, J., and Penoyre, J. *Houses in the Landscape*. Faber, 1984.

Quiney, A. *House and Home. A History of the Small English House*. BBC, 1986.

Quiney, A. *The Traditional Buildings of England*. Thames & Hudson, 1990.

Reid, R. *The Shell Book of Cottages*. Michael Joseph, 1986.

Smith, P. *Houses of the Welsh Countryside*. HMSO, 1988.

Wiliam, E. *Home Made Homes. Dwellings of the Rural Poor in Wales*. National Museum of Wales, 1988.

Index

Aby 33
Adam brothers 38
Aldford *plate 28*
Allingham, Helen 91
Alterations *see* conversion
Ampney St Peter 16
Architects 36, 91, 92, 95
Ardington 88
Arts and Crafts 95, *plates 32, 35*
Ashbee, C. R. 91
Ashleworth 14
Back-to-earth 79
Badminton 44
Barnsley brothers *plate 35*
Baslow 79
Bastle 9
Belper 42
Bibury 30
Blaise 44-5
Bledington *plate 4*
Blythburgh *plate 20*
Bodmin Moor 30
Boscawen, George 43
Box frame 14-15, *plate 5*
Bradmore 37
Bramfield *plate 14*
Brandon 28
Brandsby 93
Brick 19-20, 74, 92; nogging 17; in regions 26-35; tax 24, 73; tiles 26
Bridgwater 30
Brooks, S. H. 83
Brown, 'Capability' 38
Brunskill 35
Bunbury *plate 18*
Buscot *plate 32*
Bylaws 91, 92
Caerhays 4
Canals 36, 42-3
Carr, John 37, 42
Carving 13
Chalk 19, 74
Chambers, William 38
Chiddingstone 27, *plate 19*
Chippenham 37
Classical 44, 86 7; neo , 38, 42
Clay lump 27-8, 74
Close studding 15, *plate 2*
Clough, A. H. 96
Clunch 19, 28, 30
Coalbrookdale 32
Cob 18, 30, 74, *plate 10*
Cobble 35, *plate 16*
Collyweston 32
Compton *plate 29*
Conversion 8-10, 13, 20, 75-6, 95, *plate 24*
Cost 29, 47, 87
Cotswolds 18-20, 29, *plates 32, 34, 35*
Cottage industry 12
Cottage ornée 44, 82
Cottagers, *see* labourers, occupiers
Cowden *plate 3*

Cromford 42
Crucks 14, *plate 1*
Cymmer 4
Dance, George 42, *plate 11*
Darsham *plate 31*
Davie, W. Galsworthy 91
Dawber, Guy 91
Dean, Forest of 30
Devonshire, Duke of 44
Documentary sources 101
Dymock 14, *plate 1*
Eardisland 14
Easington *plate 16*
East Anglia 27-9, *plates 2, 6, 14*
East Malling 27
East Stratton 42, *plate 11*
Eaton Hastings *plate 34*
Eclecticism 88-9, *plate 27*
Edensor 89, *plate 27*
Elsam, Richard 40, 41, 44, 81-2
Elsecar 42
Employers 23, 47, 81
Enclosures 23, 46
Euston *plate 6*
Ffwddog 33
Flint 19, 26, 28, 30, *plate 20*
Floors 21, 74
Form, cottage 8-14, 24-5, 80, 91-7; *see also* frontage, plan
Foster, Myles Birket 91
Freeholders 23
Frontage 25, 80, 92; narrow 78, 94, *plates 21, 22*; wide 77, 99, *plate 23*
Galleting 26
George, Sir Ernest *plate 32*
Gilpin, William 39
Gimson 95
Great Milton 29
Groombridge *plate 8*
Haddenham 18
Hall house 8
Harbrow, Messrs 92
Harewood 37
Hartington *plates 9, 22*
Henley on Thames 31
Heptonstall *plate 17*
Holkham 87
Holmpton 20
Horsham stone 27
Houghton Hall 37
Howard, Ebenezer 95-6
Ham 85, *plate 26*
Investment 23, 91
Ironbridge 75, 86
Jetties 15-16, *plate 2*
Joists 16, 21, 73
Kent, Nathaniel 39-40
Labourers 7, 12, 24, 46-7, 90; *see also* occupiers
Laithe 34
Landowners 24, 36, 47, 81
Langley Park 44
Large framing 15
Lavenham *plate 2*

Leigh *plate 30*
Letchworth 91
Lethaby 95
Lewes 26
Limestone 5, 20-1, 29-30
Limpley Stoke 41, 42
Little Dawley 75
Llansantffraid 76
Llanvetherine 6, 75-6, *plate 24*
Lockinge 88
Longhouse 9-10, 35
Loudon, John 82, 88
Lowther 38
Lutyens, Edwin 91
Lyme Regis 44
Malton, James 39
Mansard 4, 28, 96, *plate 13*
Marford 43-4, *plate 12*
Materials, local 48, 91-2; mixture of 20; processed 48; regional 26-35
McVicar, J. Young 82
Mercer 77
Miller, Francis 84, 85
Milton Abbas 38
Minehead *plate 10*
Mud and stave 18
Nash, John 36, 45
Nuneham Courtenay 37, 39
Occupiers 7, 23, 36; *see also* labourers
Old Warden 85
Orford *plate 7*
Ornament 43, 94, 96
Outshut 11, 13, 33, 42
Owner occupiers 24, 47, 81
Painswick *plate 35*
Pargeting 17
Partitions 22
Patrington *plate 21*
Pattern book 37, 39-41, 81-5
Paxton, Joseph 89
Pebbles 28
Pembridge *plate 5*
Penshurst 15
Phocle Green 77, *plate 23*
Picturesque 39, 43-5, 84-9, 90, 91, *plates 25, 26*
Pisé 30
Pitched stone 33
Plans, cottage, adapted 6; formerly grand 9-11; late 92-4, 96; polite 40, 42, 43, 83, 84, 85, 86; survey 99, true cottage 13; vernacular 24, 27, 28, 31, 34, 74-9; *see also* form, frontage
Plaster 17, 21, 25
Pontymoile 43
Population 7, 23, 24, 46
Post and truss 11
Postans, Thomas 82
Potterne 79
Prefabrication 16, 92
Price, Uvedale 39
Public Health Act 90

Purlin 16, 17
Railway 48, 73, *plate 31*
Rent 29, 47
Rhostryfan *plate 15*
Roberts, Henry 82-4
Robertson, John 89
Robinson, P. F. 85
Roof, finishes 20; structure 16
Scott, Baillie 95
Scott, G. G. *plate 26*
Selworthy 84-5, *plate 25*
Services 12, 95
Shelton 86
Shingles 21
Simon, James 84, 85
Slates 20-1, 31, 32; Welsh 33, 34, 73, 74
Small framing 15
Soane, Sir John 44
Somerleyton 85
SPAB 91
Speculative builders 47
Squatters 12, 23, 47, 75

Stamford 32
Standard of living 7, 23, 95
Stoke-by-Nayland 28
Stone 18-19, 21, 74; *see also* flint, Horsham stone, limestone
Stone, Glos *plate 33*
Stonesfield 92
Surveying 98
Swithland 32
Telford, Thomas 86
Thatch 20, 27, 28, 74
Through passage 10, 11
Thrumpton 37
Tiles 21; pan- *plates 20, 21*; plain *plates 7, 8*; tilehanging 27
Timber frames 14-15, 17, 18, 31, *plates 5, 6, 14*
Tregavarras 94
Tumbling-in 20, *plate 16*
Turnpike 36, 42-3
Tyringham 44

Uckfield 4
Undivided houses 10-11
Upwey 99
Voysey 95
Wales 33
Walton-on-Thames 75
Wattle and daub 17
Wealden house 8, 9 *plate 3*
Weatherboarding 26, 27, 28
Weaver, Lawrence 90
Weavers, cottages for 34, 73, *plate 17*
Weobley 14
Wichert 18
Williams-Ellis, Clough 91
Willington 87
Windows 22, 73, 74
Windsor 44
Winster 48
Woburn 87
Wood, John 40
Wormingford *plate 13*